PRAYER IN THE RELIGIOUS TRADITIONS OF AFRICA

AYLWARD SHORTER

OXFORD UNIVERSITY PRESS
New York and Nairobi

To Sister Ancilla Kupalo and Fellow staff
members of the Pastoral Institute of
Eastern Africa, Gaba, 1968-1973

© OXFORD UNIVERSITY PRESS 1975

Library of Congress Catalogue Card Number: 75-45786
First American Printing, 1976
Printed in the United States of America

TABLE OF CONTENTS

Preface

Acknowledgements

Part one—the prayer literature of Africa

1. Nature and function of prayer in African societies   1
2. The problem of methodology in the study of African traditional religion   4
3. The basis for a typology of African prayer   8
4. The occasion, purpose and thematic infrastructure of African prayer   14
5. The style and structure of African prayer   19
6. Materialized, corporal and ritual prayer   21
7. Historical and other human factors in African prayer   23

Part two—presentation of the texts
1. The divine governance

Introduction   29

    1   Prayer to the Ancient God   30
    2   Praising the Creator of a new-born child   31
    3   Divine guidance in human work   32
    4   Prayer to become like God   33
    5   Consecration of the newborn child   33
    6   The spirituality of God   34
    7   The divine paradox   34
    8   The Hound of Heaven   35
    9   God's inescapability   35
    10   Man's creaturely insignificance   36
    11   Prayer to the Creator, the Father of Laughter   37
    12   Prayer to the King of the Gods   37
    13   Praise of the Master of Fate   38

14	Praise of God's divinatory power	38
15	The service of the Creator	39
16	Praise of the Creator's splendour	39
17	The creed of Creation	40
18	The grandeur of God, the Creator	40
19	God bewilders his people	41
20	Prayer of joyful assurance	42
21	Dancing before the Lord	43

2. The transmission and continuity of life

Introduction		44
22	Formula of blessing	45
23	The rivers of life	45
24	Life of cattle, life of men	46
25	Giver and refuser of life	47
26	Children, the field that we share with God	47
27	To the one who has power of life and death	48
28	Sow the seed of offspring with us	49
29	The life that animates the universe	49
30	Great Man, you will come back	50
31	'Planting' the dead	51
32	He who holds out his hands dies not	51
33	Fecundity and immortality	52

3. Earth, the fertile mother of living things

Introduction		52
34	May we bear children and cattle	53
35	A blessing and a curse	53
36	To the Hill Deity who gave me birth	54
37	Prayer to the Earth Goddess at the birth of a child	55
38	O Mother, deliver us	56
39	Earth, I depend upon you	56
40	The forgotten God	57
41	Prayer of the New Year festival	57

42 Prayer of the Gunnu ritual   58
43 Prayer of the Tsoede ritual   58
44 Prayer for the maturity of girls and crops   59

4. Health and healing

Introduction   60

45 Overcome all these troubles   60
46 Friend, God, we tell you about this wound   61
47 You are called to join with them in the evil   61
48 Prayer against fever and illness   62
49 Thou art the only one   63
50 Drive away the black god   63
51 May you spit upon us the medicine   64
52 May we not be tormented with maladies   64
53 May sickness be slight   65
54 Help us through these roots   65
55 Go and loose the captives' fetters   66

5. Memorial

Introduction   67

56 Blessing for a new homestead   68
57 Prayer for rain under God's tree   68
58 We know that you are with us   69
59 Prayer of my ancestors, you are spoken now   70
60 Prayer for entering a new house   71
61 Unceasing guardians of the living   71
62 A foretaste of heaven   72
63 Dream visit to the holy place   73

6. Mediation and reciprocity

Introduction   73

64 Receive our fellow who has died   74

65 Because there is hunger, you caused theft   75
66 We can only speak your names   76
67 We are your people   76
68 Our forefathers who are in your arms   77
69 We are here in your compound   77
70 Why should we be afraid of you?   78
71 If we were not present, who would feed you?   78

7. Gratitude, a foundation for trust

Introduction   79

72 I am your warrior   80
73 You have given me all   80
74 Thanksgiving for the birth of a child   81
75 Never can we thank you for your deeds   81
76 This is the story of your grace   82
77 Feeder who brings me up   83
78 The great worth of a newborn child   83
79 Divinatory harvest prayer   83

8. Conversion, forgiveness and purification

Introduction   84

80 Prayer for strength and salvation   86
81 Prayer for the conversion of the unfaithful   86
82 Divinity, heartbroken because of man   87
83 Contrition for pride and greed   88
84 How have I wronged you?   89
85 Avert this evil   89
86 We did not rob a man to build   90
87 Prayer for purity   91
88 Come and save me because I am humble   91
89 Cursing and forgiving the prodigal son   92
90 Negative confession   93
91 Wherein have we erred?   94
92 General confession   94

93	How has he erred?	96
94	Plea for forgiveness	97
95	Prayer of the prisoners	97
96	The shoulders get tired of carrying sins	98
97	Litany of the thirteen questions	99

9. Judgement

	Introduction	100
98	Let us not run the world hastily	101
99	Good morning to you, God, I am learning	101
100	You will pass before a searching judge	102

10. Protection from evil

	Introduction	103
101	Stop the wicked man	104
102	It is you who protect the home	104
103	We are in your hands	105
104	Exorcism of the cattle kraal	105
105	Let others be done by as they did	106
106	Leave me not behind, Jesus, wait for me	106
107	Protection in the rains and harvest	107
108	Hearken to my constant prayer	108
109	Purification of the forest	109
110	Hatch us, wondrous hen	109
111	The need for protective grace	111

11. Celestial symbols of prosperity and good fortune

	Introduction	111
112	The cloud-spotted sky has heard	112
113	Bring riches today as the sun rises	114
114	Prayer to the moon for luck	115

115   Prayer to the moon for success in hunting   115
116   Prayer to the moon for immortality   116
117   Prayer to the young moon   116
118   Who does not look on beauty soon is poor   117
119   Prayer for good fortune   118
120   God has given me good luck   119
121   Prayer to the new moon   119
122   Open the windows of heaven   120
123   Prayer for the good fortune of work   120

12. Peace, internal and external

Introduction   121

124   Let me pass the day in peace   122
125   Let me pass the night in peace   122
126   O God, lead my steps   123
127   Litany for peace   125
128   Prayer against unpleasant surprises   126
129   Let the souls of thy people be cool   126
130   Are our voices one ?   127
131   Prayer for Christian unity   127
132   Peace between buyer and seller   128

13. Victory and war

Introduction   129

133   Help us keep our enemies at bay   129
134   Battle hymn   130
135   Let not our town be spoiled by war   131

14. Crisis and desperation

Introduction   132

136   Prayer of the Meru exodus   133

137	Prayer for the release of death	133
138	Divinity, help me	134
139	Prayer of the sick man	134
140	Desperate plea for offspring	135
141	Prayer of the desperate hunter	136
142	Prayer for rain	136
143	I lie down without food	137
144	Prayer of the unsuccessful rain-maker	138

15. Old age and death

Introduction		138
145	The gates of the underworld are closed	139
146	Prayer for a happy old age	140
147	A long farewell	140
148	Prayer for a happy death	141
149	We are bereft of a leader	141
150	Wait awhile in life	142
151	God, you have called too soon	142
152	Give me another year, lord	143

Bibliography	144

PREFACE

This book owes much to a seminar that I helped to run in 1970 at The Pastoral Institute of Eastern Africa, Gaba. The papers of this seminar were put together in the form of a mimeographed report (strictly *pro manuscripto*) entitled *Divinity, Prayer and Oathing*. Also in 1970, I produced a small, mimeographed anthology of African prayers for private circulation, entitled *The Word that Lives*. Finally, in 1972 I contributed an article to the *African Ecclesiastical Review* on 'Prayer in African Tradition'. The fact that these activities aroused considerable interest, particularly in the shape of demand for the mimeographed anthology, ensured their being followed by a published book. I hope that the present volume will be of equal interest to social anthropologists, students of comparative religion, readers of literature, liturgical specialists and historians. My hope is also that the general reader, inside Africa as well as outside the continent, will learn more about the riches of the African religious tradition.

I wish to record my thanks to Professor John S. Mbiti of Makerere University, Kampala, for the interest and encouragement he has given me in my study of African prayer literature. I would also like to thank Rev. Andrew Walls of the University of Aberdeen for his invitation to speak in the Department of Religious Studies on the subject of African prayer. This lecture and the discussion that followed proved a very useful discipline for me at the time when I was putting the book together, and I owe some insights and modifications to contributions made on that occasion. My thanks go also to my colleagues, the staff members of the Pastoral Institute of Eastern Africa, who have shown a continued interest in my study of African prayer, both by their comments and by their frequent consultations on the subject.

Finally, I wish to thank Mr. Gerald M. T. Luyinda, who assisted me in collecting the material from which the selection was made for this book, and whose referencing of the texts was invaluable; and also Mr. F. A. Lubowa, who helped in the preparation of the manuscript for the publisher.

December, 1973

Aylward Shorter
The Limes
Stowmarket

ACKNOWLEDGEMENTS

Permission to use the following copyright material is gratefully acknowledged:

Text nos.76,123,131 and 132 in *Afrika Bidt* by F. Pawelzik, Boekencentrum B. V., Holland; text nos.94 and 109 in *Religion in an African Society* by R. T. Parsons, E. J. Brill of Leiden, Holland; text no.28 in *Kilimanjaro and Its Peoples* by C. Dundas, Frank Cass & Co. Ltd; text nos.11,104 and 118 in *African Poetry* and *Yoruba Poetry*, both edited by U. Beier, Cambridge University Press; text no.60 in *The Bakitara or Banyoro* by Roscoe, Cambridge University Press; text nos.33,44,70,71 and 79 in *The Religion of the Central Luo*, East African Literature Bureau, Nairobi; text nos.10,87 and 106 in *No Longer at Ease* and *Arrow of God* by Chinua Achebe, William Heinemann Ltd., text no.17 in *African Religions and Philosophy* by J. S. Mbiti, Heinemann Educational Books Ltd.; text no.95 in *No Easy Task* by A. Kachingwe, Heinemann Educational Books Ltd.; text no.75 in *A Woman in Her Prime* by A. Konadu, Heinemann Educational Books Ltd.; text no.137 in *Origin East Africa* edited by D. Cook, Heinemann Educational Books Ltd.; text nos.66 and 67 in *The Ngoni of Nyasaland* by M. Read, International African Institute; text nos.3, 22,34,35,45,80,81 and 136 in *The Mugwe, a Failing Prophet* by B. Bernardi, International African Institute; text nos.39 and 50 in *African Worlds* edited by D. Forde, International African Institute; text nos.30,31 and 61 in *African Systems of Thought* edited by M. Fortes and G. Dieterlen, International African Institute; text nos.69 and 93 in *Witchcraft, Sorcery and Social Categories* by A. Harwood, International African Institute; text no.42 in *Black Byzantium* by S. F. Nadel, International African Institute; text nos.20,21,62,63,77,96 and 110 in *Bantu Prophets in South Africa* by B. Sundkler, International African Institute; text no.51 in *The Bantu of North Kavirondo*, vol.I by G. Wagner, International African Institute; text nos.64 and 84 in *Rituals of Kinship among the Nyakyusa* by M. Wilson, International African Institute; text nos.65,92 and 116 in *Communal Rituals of the Nyakyusa* by M. Wilson, International African Institute; text nos.37, 85 and 86 in *More than Once* by C. Agunwa, Longman Group Ltd.; text nos.15,16,27,38,72,146,147 and 148 in *Olódùmaré, God in*

Yoruba Belief by E. B. Idowu, Longman Group Ltd.; text no.112 in *Karimojong Politics* by N. Dyson-Hudson, Clarendon Press; text nos.8,23,46,129 and 134 in *Nuer Religion* by E. E. Y. Evans-Pritchard, Clarendon Press; text no.108 in *The Nandi—Their Language and Folklore* by A. C. Hollis, Clarendon Press; text nos.24,25,47,48, 59,82,83,102,138 and 139 in *Divinity and Experience* by R. G. Lienhardt, Clarendon Press; text nos.55,97 and 152 in *African Independent Church* by H. W. Turner, Clarendon Press; text nos.40, 41,119 and 130 in *Religion and Medicine of the Ga People* by M. G. Field, Oxford University Press, London; text nos.72 and 133 in *My People of Kikuyu* by J. Kenyatta, Oxford University Press, Eastern Africa; text no.111 in *Age, Prayer and Politics in Tiriki* by W. H. Sangree, Oxford University Press, London and Makerere Institute of Social Research (then East African Institute of Social Research); text nos.5 and 101 in *Personnalité Africaine et Catholicisme*, Presence Africaine, Paris; text nos.49,90 and 103 in *Pagan Tribes of the Nilotic Sudan*, by C. G. and B. Z. Seligman, Routledge & Kegan Paul Ltd.; text nos.42 and 107 in *Nupe Religion* by S. F. Nadel, Routledge & Kegan Paul Ltd.; text nos.56,57,58,127 and 128 in *Facing Mount Kenya* by J. Kenyatta, Martin Secker & Warburg Ltd. and text no.113 in *Concepts of God in Africa* by J. S. Mbiti, The Society for Promoting Christian Knowledge, London; text no.1 in *Galla Verskunst. Ein Beitrag Zur Allgemeinen Verskunst nebst metrische Ubersetzungen* by Enno Littmann, J. C. B. Mohr (Paul Siebeck) Tübingen; text nos.7, 62,116 and 142 in *Der Ursprung der Gottesidee* by W. Schmidt, Verlag Aschendorff, Münster; text no.145 in *Les Pygmées de la Forêt Equatoriale* by R. P. Trilles, Librairie Bloud et Gay, Paris; text nos.26,68,89,100, 120,121,135,140,143,150 and 151 in *African Ideas of God* by E. W. Smith, Lutterworth Press; text nos.36,52 and 105 in *Biblical Revelation and African Beliefs* edited by K. A. Dickson and P. Ellingworth, Lutterworth Press.

NOTE: As far as possible the original text, as translated, recorded and published by the author is given. This accounts for inconsistencies in the spelling of names, and in the usage of the archaic second person singular. In some cases, I have arranged the texts in verse form and altered punctuation. I have also occasionally omitted explanations in parentheses where I judged these to be superfluous and to interrupt the text unnecessarily.

PART ONE

The Prayer Literature of Africa

1. NATURE AND FUNCTION OF PRAYER IN AFRICAN SOCIETIES

Prayer is the central phenomenon of religion, and, although the study of religion has received increasingly serious attention from social anthropologists, it would seem that less than justice has been done by them to the subject of prayer. For Heiler, author of the great classic on prayer,[1] prayer expresses the faith, life, work and ruling motive of the religious believer. It is a sign of religion wherever it is alive—religion in action—and through it differing cultural identities are revealed. But the social anthropologist working in Africa has too often described the phenomenon of prayer in terms of a secondary social or socio-psychological function, or at least as something incomplete.

For some, prayer is indistinguishable from verbal magic. The protective power with which prayer is credited is emphasized, for instance against evil and misfortune.[2] Another viewpoint is that prayer provides a form of control over one's environment, in the absence of an adequate body of empirical knowledge. According to this argument, the spirits and divinities take the place of scientific hypotheses, and the kind of communication constituted by prayer enables man to acquire an understanding of, and a control over, his environment.[3] Even Lienhardt, with his masterly study of Dinka religion[4] and his copious and carefully recorded texts of invocations and prayers, offers us no more than a sophisticated version of the 'control hypothesis'. According to him, the oral rites of the Dinka of Sudan assert a relationship between freedom and contingency in human life, a relationship in which freedom appears to be eventually stronger. Dinka prayer therefore, is a combination of an admission of weakness and an assertion of control.

A more clearly sociological hypothesis is the one which sees prayer— and particularly prayer to the ancestors—as a simple extension of hierarchical relationships. According to this explanation, the spirits

---

1. Heiler 1932, p.xiii.
2. Sangree 1966 describes this no doubt important aspect of prayer in Tiriki (Kenya), but to the exclusion of all others (cf.p.206)
3. Beattie and Middleton 1969, p.xviii.
4. Lienhardt 1961, p.251.

and divinities are presented as personalizations of the different levels of social relationship, and prayer as a means of asserting and inculcating respect for jural authority. Thus the descendants continue to feed the ancestors and to consult them as if they had been elders who were still alive. Without either wishing to deny this aspect of prayer in Africa, or to suggest that the veneration of ancestors is necessarily incompatible with theistic belief, it must be conceded that this is a minimalist explanation. The evidence shows that ancestral spirits are esteemed in the human memory for their personal worth, and that spirits who are the object of such veneration are deemed to be more powerful than the living, both in the scope of their awareness and mastery of time, as well as in the scope of their relationships. African prayer in general, and ancestor veneration in particular, are without doubt examples of prayer in its truest and fullest meaning.[1]

Although his analysis is psychological, Heiler offers a definition of prayer that is ultimately sociological. 'Prayer is a living communion of the religious man with God (conceived as personal and present in experience), a communion which reflects the forms of the social relations of humanity.'[2] If prayer were merely a speech or communication, the vehicle for a mutual sharing of thoughts and minds, this would be a social phenomenon. It is much more. It is, in Heiler's words, 'a living communion', a dimension of life itself. Prayer is not simply the oral aspect of worship or religious ritual, nor even simply an 'oral rite'. It is the essential activity, or the essential disposition of the religious man. Prayer is the basis and foundation of worship, and worship—in its usual connotation—goes beyond the verbal, material and corporal expression of prayer, to include instrumental or 'sacramental' rituals as well as merely expressive and instructional elements.

To speak of prayer in the religious 'traditions' of Africa is a little invidious and it is easy to share Professor Idowu's misgivings about the term.[3] 'Tradition' must be understood in the sense of something living and dynamic, a movement in which the continuities are more important than the discontinuities, in which new areas of application are discovered and new developments take place. The term 'indigenous' is obviously comprehensive enough to include the newer developments

---

1. Young 1950, p.156, holds the view that African ancestor veneration is not religious; so does Kopytoff, refuted by Brain (cf. Brain 1973).
2. Heiler 1932, p.358.
3. Idowu 1973, pp.103-7.

and the appropriation by Africa of religious traditions that originated outside the continent, but 'indigenous religion' might suggest a lack of historical depth. 'Primal religion', although less objectionable than 'primitive religion' is, nevertheless, not entirely free of 'fossil' overtones. The term 'tradition' will therefore be retained, bearing in mind that it is used and understood in the widest possible sense.

Heiler, writing more than forty years ago, was not embarrassed by the term 'primitive'. Primitive prayer, the prayer of pre-literate peoples, was for him the prototype of all prayer. However, there were other more sophisticated kinds of prayer, and among these were mystical and prophetical prayer. Mystical prayer took the form of self-forgetting adoration and ecstatic praise, while prophetical prayer was the transcendence of this life in this life—the prayer for salvation. For Heiler, prophetical prayer was the ideal and he saw this ideal as a development of primitive prayer and a reawakening of its vitality. Preoccupied with the psychological origins of prayer, Heiler saw an evolution from the 'naive egotism' of primitive prayer to the higher forms. 'Necessity teaches man to pray' and 'to pray is to wish.'[1] Prayer is born in times of individual need, then it becomes a regular practice in order to anticipate needs that are repeated. Prayer is basically petition, but thanksgiving is a further expression of man's conscious dependence upon supernatural powers. Finally, self-accusation and penitential prayer are used to buttress the petition and reinforce the plea, acting as a form of persuasion.

Although one agrees with the importance and meaning that Heiler attaches to prophetical prayer, it is not true to state that the religious traditions of Africa do not reveal this aspect of prayer, as well as some elements of mystical prayer. Moreover, one may be forgiven today for being indifferent to the hypothetical origins of prayer, and for refusing to believe that the prayer of pre-literate peoples can be discussed largely in terms of self-centred petitions in times of need.

Heiler, however, was right to see prayer as a communication, and as a communion. In the search for a confirmation and enrichment of his life, the worshipper surrenders and opens to another person or to other persons. Prayer introduces the worshipper to another's consciousness; it awakens him to a new understanding of reality. Prayer becomes a growth in awareness, involving increasing commitment and even risk.

---

1.   Heiler 1932, p.3.

For this reason it is frequently characterized by a certain assurance and a certain resignation. Above all, prayer is essentially an asymmetrical relationship with a supernatural power perceived in experience. It is the certainty that the power is listening to the worshipper's story as it unfolds that encourages him to speak and to develop in a way he could not do outside this experience. The one who listens has an effect upon the worshipper analagous to that of the psychotherapist upon his client, helping him more effectively through listening than through offering advice.[1] Yet, at the same time, the worshipper is also listening, becoming conscious of the change that is being worked in him.

Thus, prayer becomes a dimension of life that transcends and re-interprets every social relationship and social experience. It differs substantially from techniques of auto-salvation, such as magical rites, even though an individual may have recourse to both kinds of action by turns. Ultimately, prayer is a continuous mode of living, a living communion, by no means limited to occasions of formal utterance or formal communication. Obviously, prayer, like religious faith, has different degrees of intensity. It is also true that it operates within social structures, serving a number of social purposes unrelated or incidental to its own. These things can be, and have been, profitably studied. What concerns us here is the nature, content and form of prayer, the central phenomenon in the religious traditions of Africa.

2. THE PROBLEM OF METHODOLOGY IN THE STUDY OF AFRICAN TRADITIONAL RELIGION

We have seen that prayer can be defined as a communication or a living communion with supernatural powers perceived in experience. It follows that prayer must be categorized according to the different ways in which these powers are perceived, and the different forms that relationship with them takes. In Africa, where religious traditions are extremely numerous, this means that some form of comparative analysis must be employed. This, in turn, involves us in a method-ological critique of the various approaches that have been tried or proposed.

---

1.   This analogy is made in Hollings and Gullick 1971, pp.3 and 11.

The classical approach of the social anthropologist is fiercely particularist, insisting on a thorough-going study in each and every ethnic group, and professing an almost total agnosticism in respect of any similarities or links between them. A development of this approach is the attitude of the African scholar who would postpone all attempts at systematic comparison, until a penetrating study has been made in each and every culture by an indigenous scholar, fully conversant with the languages and *mores* of the people under study.[1] The only fruit of these proposals is the isolated monograph or, at best, a symposium of particular studies within a very general field of interest. Three things can be said about the approach.

Firstly, it is obviously essential to have competent particular studies as the basis for comparison. Secondly, a completely particularist approach is not true to the facts, since the ethnic group is a category of interaction, and not simply an isolated population. It also ignores the fact that, while particular ethnic groups enjoyed political autonomy in the past and economies that were mainly self-sufficient, other aspects of their culture (especially in the sphere of religious beliefs and practice) were often widely shared with neighbouring groups. Moreover, history reveals these ethnic groups as developing, changing, coalescing and disappearing over the years. They neither were, nor are, static entities. Thirdly, so many competent particular studies have already appeared that it must be possible to take an intelligent look at them, without waiting for the seemingly hopeless dream to be realized of finding an indigenous social anthropologist in every ethnic group.

A second approach might be called the 'enumerative' approach.[2] According to this method, comparative analysis is deemed either impossible or not worthwhile, and all that is proposed is a simple enumeration of different traditions or practices. The danger of this method is easy to see. Either one becomes a 'Frazerian'[3], linking the various phenomena by superficial similarities, or there is an implicit, undeclared—and therefore, unsubstantiated—categorization. A cross between this approach and the one just described is the type of symposium in which different aspects of traditional religion are represented

---

1. Professor Idowu would not postpone systematic comparison, but would regard it as tentative (cf. Idowu 1973, p.106).
2. Examples of this method would be Parrinder 1952 and 1969, and Dammann 1962.
3. After Sir J. G. Fraser.

by particular studies.[1] This is an improvement on simple enumeration, but it may still create the illusion that the aspects treated are part of a single, basic system.

More common, perhaps, is a third approach, followed by writers who explicitly declare their faith in the basic unity and comparability of African religious traditions. Their hypothesis is based usually upon impressions gained from wide reading, travel or discussion, but it is not systematically elaborated or tested. For Professor Abraham there is a basic 'paradigm' which justifies his study of the Akan religious system as representative of all other African religions.[2] For Professor Mbiti African religions are many, but they all derive from, and subscribe to, a basic religious philosophy.[3] For Canon Taylor there is, in Africa south of the Sahara, 'a basic world view which fundamentally is everywhere the same',[4] while for Professor Idowu there is a 'common factor' or 'common Africanness' behind African religion.[5] Faith in, or intuition of, this common unity then allows these authors to enumerate instances on grounds of similarity.

A fourth approach would appear to be more productive of tangible results. This is the method advocated by Professor Evans-Pritchard in his celebrated Hobhouse Memorial Lecture.[6] It is a limited comparative approach, according to which the differences are studied in a few religious systems, the basic cultural similarity and/or geographical proximity of which are scientifically demonstrable. Many scholars might regard his proposal as altogether too cautious, since it deepens, rather than extends, the comparative principle.

In this study of African prayer literature it is proposed to turn Professor Evans-Pritchard's method inside out, as it were, and instead of taking systems that are demonstrably similar, systems that are demonstrably diverse will either be compared or contrasted in their different approaches to common elements or themes. Such an approach must be both multi-dimensional and dynamic. It must take into account the total religious context of belief, practice, symbolism and morality, if the position of a given element or theme is to be appreciated

---

1. An example of this kind of symposium is Dickson and Ellingworth 1969.
2. Abraham 1962, p.45.
3. Mbiti 1969 and 1970.
4. Taylor 1963, p.27.
5. Idowu 1973, p.103.
6. Evans-Pritchard 1963.

within it.[1] It must definitely abandon a static view of African religion and must concern itself with the whole range of indigenous religion in contemporary Africa, not just with the religion of a hypothetical 'traditional' man.

This method would seem to be realistic, since it avoids both the agnosticism of those who say comparison is impossible or untimely and the simple faith of those who take comparison for granted. Of course, comparison is implied in categorization, but the 'plural' objective of establishing a typology against which other variables can be measured ensures that the process will provide a more realistic analysis of the facts. It does, however, involve us in the initial problem of discovering the criteria for a typology.

Two of the most promising suggestions appear to be those of Father Joseph Goetz and Professor Mary Douglas.[2] Goetz takes a socio-psychological stance, suggesting that the form which not only African but all traditional religion takes is the result of a collective psychological reaction to certain types of economy and physical environment. According to him, all religious systems can be placed somewhere along a spectrum running from extreme theism to extreme deism. In the relatively free societies of the hunter-gatherer, the shifting cultivator and the pastoralist—all passive to their environment— religion is theistic. That is to say, a Supreme Being is apprehended in a varied experience as overwhelming and multiple: in moral situa-tions, in interpersonal relationships and in the good and bad use of the created things of which he is owner and conserver. Deism, on the other hand, is the characteristic of the settled cultivator whose experience is relatively limited. It is a system in which the supreme being is acknow-ledged as the ultimate controller of life, but plays no explicit role in the daily life, nor even the formal worship of men. Very often, he is the subject of complex mythological or theological speculation. In Goetz's view, other spirits and divinities play a more or less important role against a basically theistic or deistic backdrop.

Mary Douglas takes up a more thorough sociological position. For her, the different forms of religious belief and practice are products of definable social experience, and her four categories derive from the varying strengths and combinations of group and ego-centred relation-

---

1. As we shall see, the themes may not be relevant in every instance.
2. Douglas 1970, Bergounioux and Goetz 1966.

ships.[1] Thus there are: strong theism, integrated or relative theism, deistic dualism and secularism. In many ways Mary Douglas' scheme complements and develops that of Father Goetz, but a similar criticism can be levelled at both. Helpful as they are in providing elements for an understanding of any given African traditional religious system, it is more difficult to use them as a typology. This is partly because their term of reference are necessarily general and partly because neither method takes fully into account the central religious phenomenon of prayer. The Goetz/Douglas axis of inquiry must be prolonged, to include prayer both as communication with spiritual beings and as a living communion with those same beings/aspects which we shall refer to hereafter as formal and experential prayer. Our next task is to consider the available literature and see if a number of 'prayer models' can be developed from it along these lines.

3. THE BASIS FOR A TYPOLOGY OF AFRICAN PRAYER

Before commencing the analysis, we must consider the nature of the material before us. Is it a reliable basis for such a study? A great many indigenous African prayer texts have, in fact, been collected and published, but their geographical spread is fortuitous and, what is more serious, they are not necessarily representative of the most successful studies of African religion. Not all anthropologists or ethnographers have been sufficiently interested in religion, and those that have, have not always published examples of the prayer texts they collected. This explains why there must be glaring omissions in a comparative study of prayer among African peoples.[2]

The material we have is mostly a transcription of spontaneous oral prayer, depending at most upon certain conventions of structure and phrase, but otherwise free in inspiration and composition. There are advantages and disadvantages in dealing with this kind of material. In the first place, it is what Heiler called 'primary prayer', that is, the genuine, spontaneous prayer of individuals, as opposed to 'secondary

---

1. Strong/weak group, strong/weak grid. The terms that follow in the text are mine, not Douglas'.
2. For example, J. Roscoe, the comprehensive ethnographer of the Baganda, offers us no Ganda religious texts, and even Professor Evans-Pritchard in his classic study of Nuer religion (1956) is sparing of texts.

prayer', which is formal, literary and impersonal, or which is seen as a meritorious work or a law of duty.[1] Without underestimating the value of secondary prayer, one can agree with Heiler that the primary type is closer to the real life and experience of individuals.[2] Some of the texts studied in this book have secondary characteristics. They may be texts reported out of context by informants, or they may be more stylized because of their close dependance on a ritual or musical setting. This is especially true of the prayers, hymns and religious poetry of the independent Christian churches. A few of the texts are deliberate literary compositions, either by individuals meditating on their own experience, or by African writers, putting words into the mouths of characters in their novels. In the case of ethnographers there may well be mistranslations or misinterpretations, and the most one can do is to draw attention to any informed criticism of their work which may exist. However, both the expatriate ethnographer and the African author may be tempted to dress up a text in a highly literary or poetic style.[3] In every case, a prayer text, to be understood, must be considered as part of a given, total context. It cannot be expected to be self-explanatory.

From what has been said it follows that, although a selection must be made when examples from one ethnic group, or of one type, are too numerous, the student of prayer in the religious traditions of Africa is presented with a fairly random collection of published texts which, in itself is not opposed to serious ethnographic method. All of this favours an unprejudiced, comparative study, even if one is aware of the possible limitations.[4]

Looking, then, at this material and examining each item in the context in which it is presented, one discovers at least six basic models which illustrate the underlying theology, as well as the different types of relationships to be found in formal and experiential prayer, in prayer as communication or speech, and prayer as a continuous mode of living of the believer. It cannot be too strongly emphasized that, for the African, religion is a reality or a necessity to be lived, as much as to be communicated or verbalized.

---

1. Heiler 1932, *passim.*
2. This is not the same as saying that it is individual or 'private' prayer.
3. An example is text no.108, where the ethnographer has translated the original into rhyming English verse.
4. Out of more than 300 texts collected from the published literature, 152 were retained for the purposes of this study.

The first model is one which may be called strict theism. A Supreme Being is experienced directly in life and is worshipped no less directly in formal prayer. Ancestral spirits and other spirits or divinities either play no significant role in the system, or else appear as suitors before the Supreme Being along with man himself. This model would appear to fit the Galla of Ethiopia, the Boran, Meru and Kikuyu of Kenya, the Karimojong of Uganda and the Pygmies of Zaïre and Gabon.

FIGURE 1
Strict theism

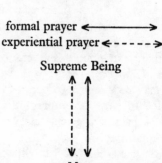

A second model is a variant of the first. In it the Supreme Being is both apprehended in life and worshipped in formal prayer through a variety of spirits, divinities or heavenly bodies, which are conceived as modes of his existence and not as independent or distinct entities. The systems of the Nuer and Dinka of Sudan and the Bushman peoples of southern Africa would appear to correspond to this model. It could be called relative theism.

FIGURE 2
Relative theism

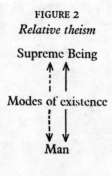

The third model is one in which divinities or spirits, usually ancestral, are seen as true and distinct intermediaries, acting not only as vehicles for man's worship of the Supreme Being, but actually mediating man's experience of him and the gift of life itself. Examples of this model would appear to include the Edo of Nigeria, the Kongo of Zaïre, the Kono of Sierra Leone, the Tumbuka of Malawi and the Nyamwezi, Kimbu and Safwa of Tanzania. This model might be called symmetrical mediation.

FIGURE 3
Symmetrical mediation

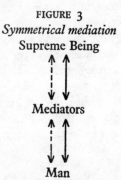

In the fourth model the mediators act principally as channels of formal prayer, and while there is little or no direct, formal worship of the Supreme Being, his own characteristic power and presence are still apparently, directly experienced and acknowledged in life. Examples seem to include the Shona of Rhodesia, the Luba and Ngombe of Zaïre, the Mende of Sierra Leone, the Chagga and Luguru of Tanzania, the Nandi and Kamba of Kenya, the Dogon of Mali and the Zande of Sudan. Possibly also, some of the peoples of Botswana and Lesotho might be included. This model could be called asymmetrical mediation.

FIGURE 4
Asymmetrical mediation

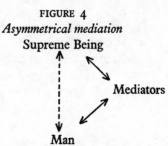

The fifth model represents strict deism in which the religious reality of a Supreme Being is thoroughly problematical. While a bond of formal worship and life-experience unites man to certain spirits or divinities, it is unclear how far a Supreme Being underlies such phenomena in the believer's thinking, let alone has any relevance for the life of mankind. Generic terms applied to the spirits or divinities do not appear to represent an independent, personalized existence. This model would appear to be rare in Africa, and virtually the only candidates in the material studied would appear to be the central Luo of Uganda, as described by Dr. Okot p'Bitek, in particular, the Acholi.[1] We are obviously on the borders here of secularism. However, there is still a cult, still formal prayer, however tenuous and circumscribed it may be. If secularism is to be partly defined by the absence of formal prayer, it stands to reason that there will not be a secularist model emerging from a study of prayer literature. Yet it is interesting to note in passing that Mary Douglas found only one African candidate for her secularist model, the Hadza of Tanzania.[2]

FIGURE 5
Strict deism

Supreme Being
?

Spirits or Divinities

Man

Finally, a very common sixth model represents relative deism; the situation in which man conceives his life as controlled by guardian divinities, spirits, heroes or eminent ancestors to which also his formal prayer is mostly directed. This relationship, however, does not rule out the direct experience and worship of a Supreme Being whose own relationship to the divinities in question, if not equivocal, is at least

1. Okot p' Bitek 1971.
2. Douglas 1970.

considered tense in some way. For example, it may even be doubtful how far the Supreme Being is, in fact, supreme; or the divinities may have been subjected to the Supreme Being only after a rebellion. This model tends further towards theism than the last, but the presence of the divinities must preclude its classification as theistic. In addition, mediation does not appear to be a prominent feature. This model might apply to the systems of the Nyoro and Soga of Uganda, the Shilluk of Sudan, the Hottentots and Ovambo of southern Africa, the Akan, Ga and Ewe of Ghana, the Ibo, Yoruba, and Nupe of Nigeria and the Ngoni of Malawi. Possibly also, the model might be found helpful in the case of the religion of the ancient Egyptians.

FIGURE 6

Relative deism

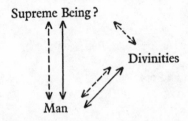

From the material studied, no clear case of dualism emerged. The only candidate was the religion of the Luyia of Kenya who invoke a good or 'white' god against an evil or 'black' god.[1] However, closer inspection reveals an asymmetrical relationship, and the Luyia should probably be classified with the theistic systems.

No doubt, intermediate models could be found. There will be differences of opinion also as to the application of these models to particular ethnic groups. Nevertheless, they offer a basic typology for formal and experiential prayer which is useful but subject to improvement. We must now consider the other possible variables in African prayer.

---

1. cf. text no.50.

4. THE OCCASION, PURPOSE AND THEMATIC INFRASTRUCTURE OF AFRICAN PRAYER

We have seen that fundamental ideas about man's relationships with spiritual beings in life and worship must strongly influence prayer, colouring the attitudes and preoccupations of the worshipper. On the other hand, human beings share basically similar life situations that form, as it were, the 'raw material' of prayer, and they tend to react prayerfully to these situations in a limited number of ways. Prayer texts can therefore be classified according to the occasions which give rise to formal prayer[1], and according to the dominant purpose in formal prayer. Looking at the material, it was possible to identify the following recurring life-situations for both individuals and communities:

(a) Childbirth.
(b) Rites of passage at puberty and on other occasions (e.g. territorial rites of passage, rites for house-building, travelling etc.).
(c) Weddings.
(d) Sickness and epidemics.
(e) Death, mourning, old age.
(f) Planting.
(g) Hunting-gathering expeditions.
(h) First-fruits of harvest or hunt.
(i) Famine.
(j) Drought.
(k) War.
(l) Reconciliation and peace.
(m) Divinatory rituals, witch-finding etc.
(n) Times of day, e.g. sunrise, midday, sunset.
(o) Seasons, e.g. new moon.

Strictly religious rituals are not included as occasions of prayer, since ritual—and especially sacrifice—is an extension of prayer itself. More will be said about ritual prayer in a later section.

---

1. Formal prayer obviously reflects experiential prayer, but some of the texts are religious prose or poetry which are not actually an invocation of spiritual beings, but a reflection or expression of experiential prayer.

The following types of dominant purpose in prayer were discernible in the texts:

(a) Petition.
(b) Intercession (or altruistic petition—on behalf of others).
(c) Thanksgiving.
(d) Praise.
(e) Confession, contrition and amendment.
(f) Purification from defilement (often related to confession).
(g) Blessing.
(h) Cursing.
(i) Lament.
(j) Forgiveness.
(k) Vows or promises.
(l) Divination.
(m) Commemoration.

Invocation is not included in the list, because it seems to be merely a stage in the unfolding of any prayer through which the worshipper calls the attention of the one he is addressing. This is not intended to minimize the great importance attached to the act of naming a person in Africa, which is regarded as affecting him personally, even rendering him personally present in a mysterious way. In this there may be magical overtones.[1] However, there does not seem to be a counterpart in African tradition to the Indian 'prayer of the name' by which a name is incessantly repeated, without any other formula. Heiler presents 'complaint' to be a dominant aspect of prayer, but this seems doubtful.[2] While lament is the prayerful expression of sorrow, complaint and questioning appear to be anthropomorphic ways of outlining the problem which is the subject of prayer, whether it be petition, intercession or confession. The question of anthropomorphisms in prayer will, in any case, be dealt with separately later on in section 7. Divination may sound odd in the context of prayer, but in some African communities it seems to be connected with the foreknowledge and mastery over time of the Supreme Being and other spiritual beings. Prayer may be thought of as a way in which these beings can reveal their hidden purposes. Once again, this will be dealt with in greater detail below.

---

1. cf. text no.97.
2. Heiler 1932, p.7.

One way of conducting a multi-dimensional comparison of the material would be to co-ordinate the life situations with the dominant purposes or reactions in prayer, and to study these variables in the light of the models already established. This would probably be a fruitful exercise, but it would not really carry the inquiry far enough. It would reveal how certain prayer reactions were more common in specific situations and how they were correlated with particular models. The fact is that prayer, being by definition the means by which men transcend the demands and experiences of their own lives, necessarily opens out on to a deeper level of experience and speculation. Prayer thus evolves a kind of infrastructure of its own, making its own emphases and establishing its own priorities. In answering the question: What is this prayer-text about?, it may be found that it is the model which comes to the fore. In this case the worshipper is preoccupied with theological questions about his communion with spiritual beings, their nature and role in his life and their relationship with each other as well as with himself. At other times, the subject of the text is more concerned with the interpretation of a particular life-situation, and yet on other occasions with underlining the dominant purpose of the prayer. Finally, other texts are much freer, being concerned with deduced, universal themes. It is this set of themes which, perhaps, arouses the greatest interest, since it builds on, and presupposes the others. One could refer to the four sets of themes as: Relational, Situational, Purposive and Universal.

Obviously, it is sometimes difficult to decide to which set of themes a given text belongs, and it might be possible to classify it in various ways. Every prayer also has its situation, purpose and model. All these variables must be considered in the analysis of the theme as a whole. Altogether fifteen themes were identified, distributed as follows:

(a) *Relational Themes*
    (i) The divine governance.
    (ii) Earth, the fertile mother of living things.
    (iii) Celestial symbols of prosperity and good fortune.
    (iv) Mediation and reciprocity.

(b) *Situational Themes*
    (i) Crisis and desperation (e.g. in famine, drought, sickness etc.).
    (ii) Victory and war.
    (iii) Old age and death.

(c) *Purposive Themes*
   (i) Gratitude the foundation of trust.
   (ii) Conversion, forgiveness and purification.

(d) *Universal Themes*
   (i) The transmission and continuity of life.
   (ii) Health and healing.
   (iii) Memorial.
   (iv) Judgement.
   (v) Protection from evil.
   (vi) Peace—internal and external.

While this division explains the principles at work behind the themes and identifies them as belonging to one or another type, the order is an artificial one. It is more natural to consider the actual texts themselves according to an order that takes account of logical connections between certain of the themes, regardless of their type. Thus, there is a connection between the theme of divine governance and the theme of transmission and continuity of life, between the theme of conversion, forgiveness and purification and the theme of judgement. For this reason the themes are treated in Part Two of the book in a more logical and less schematic order.

The following is a brief description of the scope of each theme according to that order, pointing out, in particular, the features that reveal a text as belonging essentially to the *genre* of prayer as it has been defined, and bearing in mind that a fuller description of each theme, together with a comparison of the texts within it, will be given in its place.

(a) *The divine governance*
This theme celebrates the spirituality and power of the Supreme Being, and also, to some extent, his role as judge and lord of historical time. On the part of man there is a joyful affirmation of service to him, openness to his will, and a sense that his work is man's work—the ultimate pattern of man's life and being.

(b) *The transmission and continuity of life*
This theme betrays the widespread conviction that possessing life implies also the ability to transmit life, and it sees the transmission of human life as having a divine dimension. It also speculates about the continuity of the individual life, about immortality and, on occasion, re-incarnation.

(c) *Earth, the fertile mother of living things*

The Earth Goddess, as a personalized divinity, is perhaps a West African phenomenon, but the symbolic—and indeed, real—link between earth and human life is a frequent subject of prayer in other parts of the continent.

(d) *Health and healing*

This theme has obviously been a strong preoccupation of traditional Africa, but what is perhaps surprising in the prayers that deal with this subject is that the spiritual powers are thought to be intimately concerned with man's health on the one hand, while, on the other, answer to prayer addressed to them is realized through normal medical treatment.[1]

(e) *Memorial*

This is really theme (b) in reverse. It concerns itself with the historical continuity of the sources of life and the founders of society. The living must be in harmony with their ancestors and must imitate them. Even in a mysterious way, their prayer is the prayer of the ancestors, this continuity being a pledge of divine favour.

(f) *Mediation and reciprocity*

This theme dwells on the duties of the living and the dead towards one another and of both towards the Supreme Being. It invokes the ideal of mutual concern and, in at least one instance,[2] of complete abandonment by the living to the power of eminent ancestors.

(g) *Gratitude, the foundation of trust*

Gratitude in the texts is very far from being a form of calculating insurance. It is often unaccompanied by any request, and it may even inspire a readiness to act in the service of the powers. It is, however, also an act of faith in the continuance of that favour for which the worshipper is grateful.

(h) *Conversion, forgiveness and purification*

The confession of sin, like the expression of gratitude in the last theme, is far from cynical, nor is it necessarily naïvely egotistical. Not only does it picture spiritual beings as concerned, even 'heart-broken'[3], over man's wrong-doing, but it emphasizes the need that men have to show forgiveness to one another.

---

1. Medical treatment in traditional Africa was often partly, mainly, or even wholly, magical or symbolical. This aspect of the treatment may have been effective as psychotherapy.
2. Text no.66.
3. Text no.82.

(i) *Judgement*

The idea of regarding the Supreme Being or the divinities as judges of men's actions is an aspect of several themes. This theme sums up the consciousness that man has of his life as a trial or as a school of learning, climaxed even by a final judgement at the gates of the dead.[1]

(j) *Protection from evil*

The desire for continuous divine protection, while it does not explain the whole of prayer, is definitely an important theme in many texts. On the one hand it takes the negative form of cursing or exorcism, on the other, it encourages the idea of life itself being a continuous prayer.[2]

(k) *Celestial symbols of prosperity and good fortune*

Beauty, and particularly celestial beauty, is an effective symbol of prosperity, but the African worshipper recognizes that his own efforts are one of the conditions of prosperity.

(l) *Peace—internal and external*

Peace, as well as divine protection, are considered by the African worshipper to be the outcome of experiential, or continuous, prayer. Social harmony ultimately derives from the internal harmony of the individual.

(m) *Victory and war*

This life situation provokes varied attitudes in prayer: confidence, courage, loyalty, the call for revenge and the desire for self-preservation.

(n) *Crisis and desperation*

A certain stark simplicity of style and sentiment unites all crisis prayer, whatever the actual circumstances may be. There is nothing very complex or varied about a cry for help.

(o) *Old age and death*

Death appears again as a judgement on life in the world, and stress is placed on preparation for death, as well as on the plea for more time.

5. THE STYLE AND STRUCTURE OF AFRICAN PRAYER

This study of African prayer does not simply deal with spoken prose texts; on the contrary, much of the material consists of religious poetry or hymns, recited or sung by the worshippers. This is important

---

1. Text no.100.
2. Referred to above as 'experiential prayer'.

because such an approach ensures that an entire range of texts devoted to praise and thanksgiving (sentiments more suited to poetry and song) are not left out, an omission that has often led to the conclusion that African prayer is mainly petitionary.[1]

There are three basic literary types of African prayer, and the texts reproduced in this book offer numerous examples of each. The first is the praise-poem, i.e. a panegyric or hymn. This is a lengthy, poetic recitation, usually concerned with praise or thanksgiving, but sometimes it is an extended invocation, narrating in detail a set of circumstances as the prelude to a petition. The second form is the litany or call-and-response prayer, in which a leader makes the invocations or intercessions and a choir or congregation takes up a formal response or refrain. The third form is the ritual formula or ejaculation. This is usually spoken and short in length, in the form of a petition, accompanying a ritual action. Although hymns and lengthy invocations may take place during religious rituals, they usually occur during breaks in the action itself. Texts which are spoken by an officiant while a ritual is actually in progress tend to be short and succinct, serving to underline or give meaning to the symbolic action, rather than to compete with it. If the lengthy poem or song tends to be more suited to praise or thanksgiving, and the short formula to petition, the litany suits all purposes, including especially penitential prayer. However, it is difficult to make hard and fast rules.

Generally speaking, African prayers, like those of other cultures, begin with an invocation or entry that takes one of two basic forms: presentation or invitation. The worshipper may present himself, and his community, with such phrases as: 'We are here in your compound',[2] 'God, we have come',[3] 'I have come to you here',[4] perhaps actually having undertaken a pilgrimage to a shrine or holy place. At other times, the worshipper invites his spirit interlocutors to come to him: 'This is the place where you will come',[5] 'You are called by my words',[6] 'Come and hear',[7] Let the great ones gather'.[8]

---

1. This important point is made by Finnegan 1970, p.167.
2. Text no.69.
3. Text no.43.
4. Text no.135.
5. Text no.31.
6. Text no.47.
7. Text no.85.
8. Text no.91.

It is rare that a petitionary prayer does not contain an attitude of praise or confidence, perhaps even a promise or vow. The typical petition structure contains, besides the invocation, the following three elements:

(a) Presentation of the problem.
(b) Petition expressing human dependence, but not excluding human action.
(c) Honour or praise rendered in the confident hope that the powers will act.

Thus, in the prayer of petition, no.46, the structure appears as follows:

Invocation: 'Friend, God, who is in this village'
Presentation: 'We tell you about this wound'
'We tell you about the fight of this lad'
Petition: 'Let the wound heal, let it be ransomed'
Honour, praise: 'As you are very great'
'For you are God of our home in very truth'.

Although, as Heiler pointed out, the kind of prayer common in Africa is more prophetical than mystical, we do find evidence of the 'prayer of silence' in African religious ritual. Examples are the silent offerings of the Pygmies of Zaïre, or the role of silence in the territorial offerings of the Kimbu of Tanzania. Michel Kayoya, the martyred Burundi priest, expresses the sentiment behind the prayer of silence in the words he puts into his father's mouth, when the latter was rebuked by his son for not taking part in the family, vocal prayer:

My son, you are under a delusion. You think we have to use formulas when we pray to Imana, our God. When I contemplate the work Imana has accomplished in my house, I have no need to tell him about it. Before him I keep silence, and I offer him in silence the house over which he has made me the head.[1]

6. MATERIALIZED, CORPORAL AND RITUAL PRAYER

As this book attempts to study the prayer literature of Africa, it is concerned therefore with the oral and, to some extent, written corpus

---

[1] Kayoya 1968, p. 46. An English translation by Aylward Shorter and Marie-Agnes Baldwin will shortly be published in Nairobi. The passage quoted is taken from this translation.

of texts. In fact, of course, speech is only one means of personal expression. There is also the varied language of symbolic action, expressed in ritual and dance. Using Bastide's categories, there is both materialized prayer and corporal prayer.[1] Materialized prayer occurs when the worshipper expresses his basic disposition through an action involving the manipulation of a material object of some kind. He may plant a stick in the ground (as in Madagascar), or throw a stone on to a pile (as among the South African Zulus) as a silent petition for help. Or he may wear ornaments and clothes which display a significant colour scheme, e.g., white and black (as do Kimbu ritual specialists in Tanzania) as a silent and constant prayer for rain. All of these practices find counterparts in the Catholic tradition of Europe in which putting up a candle or wearing a medal are forms of materialized prayer. Corporal prayer occurs when bodily actions, such as spitting, dancing or gesturing are considered by themselves to be a sufficient expression of prayer.

Symbolic action, however, may become even more elaborate, involving a whole complex of actions, a cast of actors or officiants and a combination of material objects, gestures and words both spoken and sung. Here we are in the realm of ritual strictly so called. Many of the texts studied in this book were composed and recited as part of a religious ritual, and although it is not our intention to study ritual as such, it is essential to refer to the ritual setting for an understanding of the texts. Other texts, however, are prayers in their own right, but, as frequently happens in Africa, are accompanied by gestures and postures which render their meaning more explicit. For example, the Kikuyu face their sacred Mount Kenya (Kirinyaga), as the Chagga of Tanzania face the equally venerated Kibo (Kilimanjaro), when they pray. Such bodily dispositions must be taken into account if texts are to be properly understood.

Other material conditions of prayer, such as the time of day (sunrise, sunset, midday etc.) or the seasons (the new moon, for example) may have an important bearing on the meaning of a text, since they relate to its situation, as well as possibly to its symbolism. There is, as a rule, no real distinction in Africa between individual and collective prayer. Prayer functions are frequently departmentalized according to different levels and segments of the political and social structure.

---

1. Bastide 1972, pp.106–7.

Thus the prayer of an individual is frequently and intentionally communitarian, even if it is not communitarian in expression. However as we have seen, strictly ritual prayer is more likely to be communitarian in articulation than individual prayer.

This would seem to be the place in which to say a word about the role of spirit mediumship in African prayer. As Beattie and Middleton put it: 'The mediumistic relationship is thought to be a particularly close one, more so than can be achieved through such means as sacrifice prayer or the observation of omens.'[1] There is, in fact, no inherent contradiction between spirit mediumship and genuine prayer. The phenomena of mental dissociation and glossolalia may be means of achieving that sense of self-surrender and expansion of understanding which is true prayer. On the other hand, as Beattie and Middleton also point out, the chief objective in spirit mediumship may be oracular, or it may be a form of communication or transaction with forces which have no religious significance in the lives of those who take part. Everything depends on the cultural content which is read into the activity itself.

7. HISTORICAL AND OTHER HUMAN FACTORS IN AFRICAN PRAYER

The theme which has been named 'memorial' for the purposes of this study has obvious historical overtones, and in the introduction to the theme itself there is a fuller discussion of them. It is certainly possible that prayer texts which treat this theme may provide important evidence for the history of a particular African religious tradition. On the other hand, some prayer texts (belonging to other themes) appear to be already a part of a specific historical tradition, and necessarily shed light on the historical development of religious beliefs and practices. The prayers ascribed to the founder of the Kikuyu people, for example,[2] or to the leader of the Meru exodus to Kenya,[3] provide interesting evidence of this kind. There is even, in the case of the Mende of Sierra Leone, a tradition about the origin of prayer itself.[4] Critical examination

---

1. Beattie and Middleton 1969, p.xviii.
2. Text no.72.
3. Text no.136.
4. Text no.135.

of such material by historians may well prove fruitful. On the other hand, religion is often conservative, and even prayer texts which are not explicitly historical may contain archaic references to cults, divinities and heroes that are important links in the chain of historical reconstruction. The extent to which different African religious traditions have influenced each other through historic contact will, if it can be established, be a vital factor in the comparative analysis of African religious systems, and in plotting the geographical spread of religious cults and practices.

The very spontaneity of African prayer encourages anthropomorphisms and human liberties which may appear out of place to one reared in a tradition of formalized, secondary prayer. Some prayers appear to be cynical, and others give vent to scolding or complaint Here is an example from South Africa.

> You are useless, gods!
> You are just being tiresome.
> Although we are offering you sacrifices,
> You do not answer us.
> We are deprived of everything.
> You are full of hate.[1]

At other times there is an attempt to bargain, and in a great many cases, a form of petulant interrogation: 'Why is this happening to me?', 'Why do I go hungry?', 'Wherein have I erred?' etc. In most cases these usages are simply human responses to the inscrutability of divine activity, and they are set against the background of an implicit, and even explicit, acceptance of the divine will as the outcome of prayer. The idea that prayer, if it is properly conducted and recited in all its details, must produce an infallible effect, is also quite common. If there is no answer to prayer, it is felt that there must be a mistake somewhere. The mistake may even be attributed to the spirits themselves as happened when an Ngombe (Zaïre) hunter, who had prayed for a successful hunt, only killed his quarry after some initial failure. His prayer of thanksgiving was as follows:

> Our God, we rejoice.
> We thought you had made a mistake![2]

Such an attitude may also be struggling to express human incomprehen-

---

1. Junod 1913, p.368, quoted by Bastide 1972, p.113.
2. Smith 1950, p.172.

sion, rather than violating the character of the prayer itself. It must be balanced against the overall purpose of the prayer.

Finally, there is the question of divinatory prayer. We have already mentioned the praise of divination as part of God's providence and foreknowledge. Divination, however, may even be built into prayer. The worshipper may expect an immediate answer to prayer, or a sign in the very act of worship itself that the prayer will shortly be answered. The sacrificial animal may be expected to urinate,[1] the ground may be expected to shake,[2] the offered grain may be expected to be disturbed by unseen hands during the night, or rain may be expected to fall even before the prayer asking for it is over. Human beings are tempted to look for a tangible sign of divine approval. This may be an indication of naïve confidence in the literal efficacity of prayer, but it has to be admitted that, in the measure in which it imposes conditions upon the powers, it undermines the essence of prayer as defined.

In the second part of the book we present a selection of prayer texts, grouped according to the themes which have been identified, with a general introduction to each theme and a particular introduction to each text.

---

1.   Text no. 59.
2.   Text no. 79.

PART TWO

Presentation of the Texts

1. THE DIVINE GOVERNANCE

Introduction

Not all African peoples have an idea of creation in the strict sense of creation out of nothing, and when there is a Creator, he is not always very strictly identified with the Supreme Being. Creation is an aspect of the divine governance or mastery of the world, and praise of the governor or master appears to be one of the most common themes of African prayer. This section contains twenty-one examples from fifteen ethnic groups.

Among the peoples whose religion has a theistic emphasis, mastery is directly attributed to the Supreme Being. He is clearly the Creator and source of all life—'father' and 'mother'—among the Milembwe of Zaïre. He is the powerful master for the Gabon Pygmies, and, in the thinking of the Ethiopian Galla, his power is ancient and permanent. The ubiquitous and inescapable character of this power is a recurring theme among the Susu of Guinea, the Pygmies and the Nuer of Sudan, while for the Dinka, also of Sudan, this power is a paradox of immanence and transcendence, of conjunction and division. No doubt, the idea of creation figures prominently in these prayers, but equally prominent is the aspect of conservation and concern. The Meru of Kenya, the Milembwe and Galla all stress this idea. For the Milembwe, however, the concern of the Creator for his creation is, to some extent, conditional on human fidelity to the duty of praise. Man also has a duty to work at the Creator's bidding and the Meru text implies that man's work is the Creator's work. The Susu prayer begs very simply that men may 'be like' the 'father' and 'mighty force'.

Many of the same ideas are present in the prayers of peoples with hierarchies of semi-divine heroes and tutelary gods. In spite of the inextricable relationship between their hero, Nyikang, and the Supreme Being, the Shilluk of Sudan stress the latter's ubiquity and inescapability. 'To whom shall we pray? Is it not to thee?' While the fore-knowledge and mastery over time of the oracles and oracle deities of the Yoruba of Nigeria redound to the praise of the Supreme Being, Olódùmaré. So also does the power of the Creator-deity, Orìsá-Nlà, who is the father of laughter and cause of joy. But the Yoruba Creator is also an inscrutable judge of men's actions.

For the peoples who emphasize ancestor veneration, the Supreme Being (who is also the Creator) is perhaps grander and more in-scrutable. This is clear from the beautiful, descriptive prayer of the Shona of Rhodesia, and from the ultimate causality of both good and evil attributed to the Kimbu Creator in Tanzania. Finally attitudes of creaturely insignificance and joyful affirmation are carried over from tradition into the modern prayers of the Nigerian Ibo and South African Zulu, whose content has been greatly influenced by the Bible.

1 | Prayer to the Ancient God[1]

This prayer of the Galla of Ethiopia stresses not only the permanence of the 'ancient' or 'aged' God, it also expresses God's concern to hear, see and receive his people. It expresses too, the worshipper's indiffer-ence to created things which belong first of all to God.

> Listen to us aged God
> Listen to us ancient God
> Who has ears!
> Look at us aged God
> Look at us ancient God
> Who has eyes!
> Receive us aged God
> Receive us ancient God
> Who has hands!

---

1. Littmann 1925, p.19.

If you love beautiful horses, take them!
If you love beautiful women, take them!
If you love beautiful slaves, take them!
Listen to us O God,
O God listen to us.

2 | *Praising the Creator of a New-Born Child*[1]

This prayer of the Milembwe of Zaïre is a meditation on man's relationship to God and an expression of welcome to a new-born child. After reciting God's names, the worshipper lists the peoples, lands and things created by him. God is Creator, but his concern for his creatures is conditional on their fulfilling their duty of praise.

God Almighty Creator,
God Mbunwa Mukungu a Kinyima
Created trees, created people, created all the countries,
Created the Been'Ekiiye of Kalanda, created the Beena Mpaaza and
  BaaMilembwe,
Created the Beena Musolo and Muelaayi, created the Beena Kibeeji of
  Muteeba,
Created the white and the whitish,
Created the Lomami, created the Luamba Kasseya [two rivers],
Created the land where the sun rises,
Created the fish at Msengye,
Created the eldest and youngest of a twin,
Created the guide who leads [child that opens the womb],
Created the eatable and uneatable ants.
God, thou art the Lord,
Who cometh in the roar of the whirlwind,
Out of your dwelling place from where the sun rises.

---

1. Stappers 1952, p. 6.

God Creator, thou art father and thou art mother.
O God, I should not offend you as if you were a man;
There is no gratitude for what God bestows upon you,
Although he gives you a wife who grinds maize, a woman is a basket.
A man is a refuge. When rain falls I may enter.
God, if he has not given you a gift, he will remember when you praise
  him.
Honour him and you arrive at Musengye of the Mulopwe [?].
Everyone is not a welcome guest; only a child is a stranger who comes
  quite new in our midst.
Oh eldest and youngest of a twin, only a child is welcome as a stranger
Fricnd, **good** day, friend good day!

3 / *Divine Guidance in Human Work*[1]

These three prayers were composed by Mr. M. Kamunde of the
Tharaka Meru in Kenya, a well-known medicine man. The first is an
evening prayer, the second a prayer before work, the third a prayer of
praise for the wonders of creation. God is addressed as Ngai and
Murungu.

> Ngai, you are the Lord, help me well,
> So that I may get up tomorrow
> With my limbs healthy,
> And show me the work I have to do.
>
> ———
>
> Ngai, help me that I do not see
> Any danger while I work,
> Because I know
> That there is many a danger.

---

1. Bernardi, 1959, pp.124–5.

Murungu, you created men,
And you created all the members
Of the body.
He created the mouth,
The nose, the eyes and the back.
And you created all the animals.
He creates even the monkey
Without a tail.

4 | Prayer to Become Like God[1]

A boy aged about fifteen and belonging to the Susu people of Guinea
prays this prayer before the fierce trial of courage imposed upon him
by custom—the killing of a leopard. The prayer is put into the mouth
of one of his characters by Prince Modupe.

Father, O mighty force,
That force which is in everything,
Come down between us, fill us,
Until we be like thee,
Until we be like thee.

5 | Consecration of the Newborn Child[2]

This prayer of the Gabon Pygmies accompanies the offering of a
newborn child to God, as a kind of first-fruits offering. The text
stresses the power and the mastery of God.

To you the Creator, to you the powerful
I offer this new plant,
New fruit of the old tree.
You are the master, we are the children.
To you the Creator, to you the powerful.

1. Modupe (1950) in Edwards 1963, p.32.
2. *Personnalité Africaine et Catholicisme*, 1962, p.51.

6 / The Spirituality of God[1]

This Pygmy praise-poem from Zaïre is an example of pure theism, the multiple and all-embracing experience of the supreme being. The name given to him is Kmvoum.

> In the beginning was Kmvoum,
> Today is Kmvoum,
> Tomorrow will be Kmvoum.
> Who can make an image of Kmvoum?
> He has no body.
> He is as a word which comes out of your mouth.
> That word! It is no more.
> It is past and still it lives!
> So is Kmvoum.

7 / The Divine Paradox[2]

Deng is one of the free divinities of the Dinka of Sudan, one of the personalized experiences or relationships of human individuals that make up the total experience of Divinity. Deng is associated with rain, a source of life. This prayer expresses the paradox of Divinity's nearness and farness. The 'black bull' released from 'the moon's byre' refers to the clouding over of the penumbra of the moon.

> Great Deng is near, and some say 'far'.
> O Divinity,
> The Creator is near,
> And some say 'he has not reached us',
> Do you not hear, O Divinity?
> The black bull of the rain
> Has been released from the moon's byre.
> Do you not hear, O Divinity?

1. Young 1940, p.23.
2. Nebel in Schmidt 1949, p.143.

8 | The Hound of Heaven[1]

Among the Nuer of Sudan, Deng is the greatest of the Spirits of the Air, a refraction of Spirit or Kwoth. This text is traditionally the reply made by Deng himself to the man who says he is tired of the demands that Deng makes upon him. Spirit is ubiquitous and inescapable like the air. He cannot be avoided.

> A man avoiding Deng
> Will find Deng in front,
> On the right he will find Deng,
> On the left he will find Deng,
> Behind him he will find Deng.

9 | God's Inescapability[2]

Among the Shilluk of Sudan, Nyikang, the Hero-Ancestor, is merged with the Supreme Being himself and both are invoked together. In this prayer the divine providence and omnipresence are celebrated. Also mentioned is Dak, the spirit that possesses the Shilluk king or Reth. The prayer accompanies sacrifice.

> I implore thee, thou God,
> I pray to thee during the night.
> How are all people kept by thee all days?
> And thou walkest in the midst of the grass,
> I walk with thee;
> When I sleep in the house I sleep with thee.
> To thee I pray for food, and thou givest it to the people
> And water to drink.

---

1 Evans-Pritchard 1956, p.47.
2. Westermann 1912, p.171.

The soul is kept by thee.
There is no one above thee, thou God.
Thou becamest the grandfather of Nyikango[1].
It is thou [Nyikang] who walkest with God.
Thou becamest the grandfather [of man] and thy son Dak.
If a famine comes, is it not given by thee?

So as this cow stands here, is it not thus:
If she dies does her blood not go to thee?
Thou God, to whom shall we pray?
Is it not to thee?
Thou God, and thou who becamest Nyikango
And thy son Dak.
But the soul is it not thine own?
It is thou who liftest up.

10 | Man's Creaturely Insignificance[2]

This Biblical prayer is put by Achebe into the mouth of Mary, a zealous Ibo Christian at the ceremony held before the departure for England of Obi, the hero of the novel. Local Nigerian symbolism is provided by the reference to the yam and to ants. The latter image is used by a number of African peoples to express man's creaturely insignificance before God.

Oh God of Abraham, God of Isaac and God of Jacob, the beginning and the end. Without you we can do nothing. The great river is not big enough for you to wash your hands in. You have the yam and you have the knife; we cannot eat unless you cut us a piece. We are like ants in your sight. We are like little children who only wash their stomach when they bath, leaving their back dry.

---

1. The more common form of this name is Nyikang.
2. Achebe 1960, p.9.

11 | Prayer to the Creator, the Father of Laughter[1]

In the pantheon of the Yoruba of Nigeria, Orìsá-Nlà, the Creator, is not supreme. His work of creation is subject to Olódùmaré, the King of the Gods. In this prayer he is presented as an all-knowing judge, and as the father of laughter and success. He is also Obatala, the one who gives to parents the joy of having children.

> He is patient, he is not angry.
> He sits in silence to pass judgement.
> He sees you even when he is not looking.
> He stays in a far place—but his eyes are on the town.
> He stands by his children and lets them succeed.
> He causes them to laugh—and they laugh.
> Ohoho—the father of laughter.
> His eye is full of joy.
> He rests in the sky like a swarm of bees.
> Obatala—who turns blood into children.

12 | Prayer to the King of the Gods[2]

This prayer of praise celebrates the victory of Oóldùmaré, King of the Gods, over the other divinities. According to the legend of the Nigerian Yoruba, the other gods conspired against their king, and he allowed them to rule the world without him. The result was disaster; the world came to a standstill. The gods then sang this hymn.

> Be there one thousand four hundred divinities of the home,
> Be there one thousand two hundred divinities of the market-place,
> Yet there is not one divinity to compare with Olódùmaré.
> Oóldùmaré is the King unique.
> In our recent dispute,
> Edùmaré[3] it is who won.
> Yes, Edùmaré.

---

1. Beier 1966, p.17.
2. Idowu 1962, p.55.
3. Another version of Olódùmaré.

13 / Praise of the Master of Fate[1]

Among the Yoruba of Nigeria, Ifa is an impersonal principle of divination created by Orìsá-Nlá and associated with Fate and with the providence and power of the King of Gods, Olódùmaré. This poem of praise celebrates the mastery over time which Ifa represents.

Ifa is the master of today,
Ifa is the master of tomorrow;
Ifa is the master of the day after tomorrow;
To Ifa belongs all the four days
Created by Orìsá into this world.

14 / Praise of God's Divinatory Power[2]

Eji-Ogbe is the first and senior figure in the systems of divination used by the Yoruba of Nigeria who throw seeds and interpret their patterns. Divination is associated with Olorun, the God of Heaven, another title of Olódùmaré, the King of the Gods, and this power makes him superior to them.

The might of all rivers in the world is not to be compared with
    that of the sea;
The dignity of rivers which rise on the hill is not as that of the
    lagoon.
There is no Ifa that can be compared with Eji-Ogbe;
To command is the privilege of a commander;
Eji-Ogbe, you are the king of them all.
I asked for honours from the lagoon, for he is greater than the
    river.

---

1. Abimbola 1965, pp.2–3.
2. Clarke 1939, p.248.

I received them, but I was not satisfied.
I asked them at the hands of Olokun Jeniade, the God of the sea
and father of all rivers,
But still I was not satisfied.
Who does not know that only the gifts of Olorun, the God of
Heaven,
Are sufficient till the day of one's death?

15 | The Service of the Creator[1]

In this prayer the Yoruba worshipper in Nigeria praises Orísá Nlá, the
Creator-Deity who is the minister of Olódùmaré, King of the gods.
Orìsá moulds the human body, and after Olódùmaré has breathed life
into it, sends the newly created man on his way to the world. Man is
responsible to Orìsá in the first place.

> He who makes eyes makes nose:
> It is the Orìsá I will serve;
> He who creates as he chooses:
> It is the Orìsá I will serve;
> He who sends me here:
> It is the Orìsá I will serve.

16 | Praise of the Creator's Splendour[2]

This prayer is addressed by the Yoruba of Nigeria to the Creator-
deity, Orìsá-Nlá. Although he is not the Supreme Being, he is
hailed as venerable, mighty and splendid, shining in white robes. He is
holy, kindly and authoritative.

---

1. Idowu 1962, p.72.
2. Idowu 1962, p.75.

Orìsá! The Immovable! The Noble One!
He-who-lives-in-gorgeous-greatness;
He is so mighty that he cannot be lifted;

Immense in white robes!
He sleeps in white clothes!
He wakes in white clothes.
He rises in white clothes.

Venerable Father! Yemowo's consort!
Orìsá delights me as he is in state;
It is a delectable place where Orìsá is enthroned.

17 | The Creed of Creation[1]

This communal song from the Soga of Uganda was a means by which
the teaching of the community was recalled and its belief strengthened.

God created:
He created man,
He gave him a wife
To bear children.
He created the earth,
He blesses it.

18 | The Grandeur of God, the Creator[2]

This praise-poem is addressed to Mwari, God of the Shona of Rhodesia.
Mwari is God and Creator of the Cosmos and the spirits of the dead
dwell with him. The prayer is full of imagery borrowed from the
Rhodesian landscape.

1. From a student's examination paper at Makerere University quoted by
    Professor J. Mbiti, Mbiti 1970, p.46.
2. Posselt 1942, quoted in Smith 1950, p.127.

Great Spirit,
Piler up of the rocks into towering mountains!
When thou stampest on the stone,
The dust rises and fills the land.
Hardness of the precipice;
Waters of the pool that turn
Into misty rain when stirred.
Vessel overflowing with oil!
Father of Runji,
Who seweth the heavens like cloth:
Let him knit together that which is below.
Caller forth of the branching trees:
Thou bringest forth the shoots
That they stand erect:
Thou hast filled the land with mankind,
The dust rises on high, Oh Lord!
Wonderful One, thou livest
In the midst of the sheltering rocks.
Thou givest of rain to mankind.
Hear us Lord!
Show mercy when we beseech thee, Lord.
Thou art on high with the spirits of the great.
Thou raisest the grass-covered hills
Above the earth, and createst the rivers,
Gracious One.

19 | God Bewilders His People[1]

In this song the Kimbu of Tanzania recall the great famine of about
1840 when the survivors went from village to village and from one
hill-shrine of their ancestors to another, looking for more survivors

---

1. Shorter 1972, p.253.

and found none. They were 'bewildered' by the Creator. Kimbu never pray formally to Matunda, the Creator, and their experience of the divine is usually mediated by the ancestors and territorial spirits. This famine was such an extraordinary event in their history that it was attributed to Matunda's ultimate causality.

Matunda bewildered them. Perhaps there are people.
At Ipupi's there are people. Perhaps there are people.
At Igavaansi's there are people. Perhaps there are people.
Matunda bewildered them. Perhaps there are people.
I return to Nyalanga; he confused them. Perhaps there are people.
At Lukwili there are people. Perhaps there are people.
We left Luwumbu's; there are people. Perhaps there are people.
Matunda bewildered them. Perhaps there are people.
Perhaps there are people. Perhaps there are people.
They lived thus in the forest. Perhaps there are people.
The people are wiped out. Perhaps there are people.
The great famine finished us all. Perhaps there are people.

20 | Prayer of Joyful Assurance[1]

The Zulu Nazarite or Zionist Church sings hymns that have a freshness and immediacy born of deep religious experience. In this kind of hymn, the prophet or precentor sings the verses and the people respond with chorus or key-word. The attitude of joy expressed in the hymn typifies the Zionist Churches of South Africa.

Our Father, who art in Heaven!
I am in thy kingdom.
May thy name
Be kept holy!

---

1. Sundkler 1948, p.195.

Chorus:
May thy Spirit come, O King
And give life to thy people!

21 | *Dancing Before the Lord*[1]

The sacred dance is practised by the Zulu Nazarite or Zionist Church among others in South Africa. It is an expression of joyful praise offered to God and is accompanied by invocations such as the following that God will himself strengthen the dancers.

> Great is, O King,
> Our happiness
> In thy kingdom,
> Thou, our king.
>
> We dance before thee,
> Our king,
> By the strength
> Of thy kingdom.
>
> May our feet
> Be made strong;
> Let us dance before thee,
> Eternal.
>
> Give ye praise,
> All angels,
> To him above
> Who is worthy of praise.

---

1. Sundkler 1948, pp.197–8.

2. THE TRANSMISSION AND CONTINUITY
OF LIFE

Introduction

Life and the sharing of life are such well-known, fundamental values in Africa that it is hardly surprising to find particular aspects of this theme overlapping the boundaries of the different types of religious systems. This is clearly made evident by the twelve examples in this section, coming from ten ethnic groups.

Two prayers from the more theistic systems, the Meru of Kenya and Nuer of Sudan, present a point of view which is surely more widespread, even if it is not explicitly contained in other texts of this section. This is the point of view that to live is to transmit life. If one does not have children one is not alive. The Dinka prays for the 'life of cattle, life of men', because the increase of the herd is a symbol and—through bridewealth—a means of increase in the family. He is also perturbed by the paradox that the negation of life can supervene, even after a prayer for life.

The idea that life is a sharing in the divine creativity unites the Rundi, with their more theistic approach, to the Yoruba of Nigeria, with their pantheon that includes the Creator-divinity. The same is true of the Chagga of Tanzania, although ancestor veneration is a stronger feature of their religion. The Dogon of Mali discover an intimate relationship between the ancestor spirits and the whole of creation of which they are the hierophants, or sacraments. The petition for life is directed to God through a universe in which life is the dominant force.

Among those for whom the ancestors are the primary guardians of life, we find the idea of literal reincarnation expressed by the Edo of Nigeria and a more metaphorical approach to the same idea among the Kongo of Angola and the Central Luo of Uganda. In all these societies life and the transmission of life depend upon harmonious relationships between the living and the spirits of the dead.

44

Among the Meru of Kenya the Mugwe is a prophet, leader, reformer
and law-maker who controls initiation rites and military exploits.
This blessing formula is used by the Mugwe of Imenti and is addressed
to God on Kenya, the mountain of brightness (Kirinyaga). The
blessing asked for is life and the transmission of life. The Mugwe
shows concern for other lands which fall under his responsibility.

> Kirinyaga,[2] owner of all things,
> I pray thee, give me what I need,
> Because I am suffering,
> And also my children [are suffering]
> And all things that are in this country of mine.
> I beg thee for life,
> The good one with things,
> Healthy people with no disease,
> May they bear healthy children.
> And also to women who suffer because they are barren,
> Open the way by which they may see children.
> [Give] goats, cattle, food, honey.
> And also the troubles of the other lands
> That I do not know, remove.

23 | *The Rivers of Life*[3]

The Nuer of Sudan address this prayer to Buk, mother of Deng,
Spirit of the Air. Buk is associated with rivers and streams, and as
such she is a mode of God's existence, the source of life. Deng is

---

1. Bernardi 1959, p.115.
2. Mr. J. N. K. Mugambi in a personal communication questions this usage
   of 'Kirinyaga'. According to him, 'Kirinyaga' refers exclusively to Mount
   Kenya which is not worshipped and cannot be a bilocution for the Supreme
   Being himself. Letter 27/3/1973.
3. Evans-Pritchard 1956, pp.45–6.

sometimes called by his ox-name Dengkur, and Buk is Buk Deang, 'mother of Deng'. 'She brings life and our children play.' The pied crow is Buk's bird.

> Mother of Deng, the ants ransom their lives from thee,
> Mother of Dengkur, the ants ransom their lives from thee,
> The Mother of Dengkur brings life,
> The Mother of Dengkur brings me life,
> Life is revived.
> She brings life and our children play,
> They cry aloud with joy,
> With the life of the Mother of Deng,
> With the life of the Mother of Deng,
> The pied crows are given life and are filled.
> Our speech is good, we and Buk,
> Our speech is excellent;
> The country of the people is good,
> We journey on the path of the *pake* [Fakir].
> We are here, we and Buk Deng,
> Buk, Mother of . . . . [Deng].

24 | Life of Cattle, Life of Men[1]

The herd of cattle is for the Dinka of Sudan an effective symbol of the human family and in this prayer to Divinity, life is sought for both. The 'white one' is the white ox, symbol of Divinity. Deng is the free Divinity associated with rain, son of Abuk, patroness of motherhood, of gardens and crops. He is invoked as a mediator.

> I pray the white one.
> Is Divinity not near?
> Does my father not give us life?
> Deng, son of Abuk, pray for life,
> Life of cattle, life of men.

1. Lienhardt 1961, pp.38–9

46

25 / Giver and Refuser of Life[1]

This Dinka (Sudan) prayer is addressed to Garang, who personifies the human perception of Divinity in the father-son relationship and in the heat of the human body. The red and white heifer is his emblem. Nyiwol is the great-grandfather of the worshipper, and the tethering of the bull is in preparation for sacrifice. The worshipper is preoccupied with the paradox that Garang can give and refuse life. (For Abuk cf. previous prayer.)

> Pray the red and the white.
> Life is prayed for from the red one.
> Life is prayed for, pray the red and white.
> We will appease the great one [Garang],
> We of the family of Nyiwol.
> Your bull will be tethered at its peg
> Throughout the heat of the day,
> And will you deceive me and give me life,
> And come and follow me with evil,
> My father Garang, and Abuk Deng,
> And refuse life to the ants ?[2]

26 / Children, the Field that we Share with God[3]

In Burundi mothers sing songs to their babies to quieten them, rather than to lull them to sleep. This baby song is a religious poem celebrating the idea that parenthood is a sharing in God's creativity. Imana, the Supreme Being, represents good fortune and women believe they may meet him by chance at the water's edge in the form of a calf. The singer calls her baby 'child of my mother' and even 'mother' because it is a nominal or metaphorical reincarnation of its grandmother.

1. Lienhardt 1961, p.88.
2. The Dinka humiliate themselves before Divinity by calling themselves 'ants'.
3. Guillebaud 1950, p.197.

Hush, child of my mother,
Hush, hush, O my mother!
God who gave you to me,
If only I could meet him,
I would fall on my knees and pray to him.
I would pray for little babies,
For little babies on my back.

You came when the moon was shining,
You came when another was rising,
Hush, field that we share,
That we share with Imana!
God who gave you to me,
May he also bring you up for me.

27 | *To the One Who has Power of Life and Death*[1]

The Yoruba of Nigeria call their Creator-deity, Orìsá, by the name of
Iku (death), because he has power of life and death. The worshipper
here prays for a share in the Orìsá's creativity, so that he may be
'multiplied' in many offspring.

O Death,
You who domicile with a person
And imbue him with nobility!
O Sceptre-Wielder!
O You who multiply only one into two hundred persons,
Multiply me into four hundred,
Multiply me into two hundred,
Multiply me into one thousand four hundred and sixty
    persons.

---

1. Idowu 1962, p.74.

28 / Sow the Seed of Offspring with Us[1]

This prayer was recited by the Chagga of Tanzania, facing Mount Kilimanjaro, thought to be the abode of Ruwa, God. It accompanied the sacrifice of a bull for the healing of a sick man. The bull was initially given by God to the sick man, now it is restored as 'the bull of your name'. God is addressed as 'Chief', 'Preserver', and 'Elephant', and the prayer for health turns into a petition for offspring and the continuance of the clan.

> We know you, Ruwa, Chief, Preserver,
> He who united the bush and the plain,
> You, Ruwa, Chief, the Elephant indeed,
> He who burst forth men that they lived.
> We praise you and pray to you and fall before you.
> You have sent us this animal which is of your own fashioning
> For you share with no man and none is given thereof.
> Chief, receive this bull of your name.
> Heal him to whom you gave it and his children.
> Sow the seed of offspring with us,
> That we may beget like bees.
> May our clan hold together
> That it be not cleft in the land.
> May strangers not come to possess our groves.
> Now, Chief, Preserver, bless all that is ours.

29 / The Life that Animates the Universe[2]

The Dogon patriarch in Mali recites this prayer during the annual sacrifice. He performs libations and immolates two chickens. The prayer is addressed to the ancestors as well as to God (Amma), those

1. Dundas 1924, p.146.
2. Dieterlen 1941, p.150.

who give life to an animated universe. The ancestors are reminded of
the things they did in life, breaking the *wolo* (kola nut?), building,
carrying water, etc. The petition is for children.

Amma, accept the morning greeting;
Things which come after Amma, accept the morning greeting;
Earth, accept the morning greeting;
Yeban, Andumbulu, Guinu [ancestors],
Kumogu [seeing] trees, Kumogu [seeing] stones,
Everything, accept the morning greeting;
You who have placed the stone, accept the morning greeting;
You who balanced the steps, accept the morning greeting;
You who set the three [stones] of the hearth,
Accept the morning greeting;
You who slept on beds, accept the morning greeting;
Women who bore long-necked calabashes,
Accept the morning greeting;
The water of our old men has gone out [the libation],
Take and drink.
If you have drunk, give me a long old age;
Give me the eight grains and the fruit of the calabash-tree for a ninth;
Make me a gift of children;
Let me reach next year.

30 / Great Man, You Will Come Back[1]

This funerary prayer is addressed to the spirit of the dead man, among
the Edo of Nigeria. It demonstrates a belief in a literal reincarnation
and asks that the next incarnation may be happier and more lengthy.

You came to the world and you lived to old age . . .
When you come back may you once again bring a good body with you.
Money, health, all the things that are used in living, you must
bring them with you . . .

1. Fortes and Dieterlen 1965, p.105.

50

When you come again may sickness not send you back.
May you not suffer the diseases of this world in your next incarnation.
Great Man, you will come back!

31 | 'Planting' the Dead[1]

Another Edo (Nigeria) funerary prayer, recited after the burial or 'planting' of a dead man. The worshipper is introducing the new guardian spirit into the house with gifts and asks life for himself and his children.

> My father, Idehen, who has slept,
> I have buried you.
> Behold the goat, the palm wine.
> Behold the four kola nuts
> That I have brought to introduce you into the house.
> This is the place where you will come and eat now.
> Let me not die.
> Let my children not die before me . . ..

32 | He Who Holds Out His Hands Dies Not[2]

This is a Kongo prayer of thanksgiving from Angola in which the ancestors are thanked for curing a patient and are shown the food and drink brought for a feast in their honour. It is also a prayer for offspring, and there is the interesting idea that prayer is a condition of immortality.

> I have held out my hands to you [in prayer],
> And he who holds out his hands dies not.

1. Fortes and Dieterlen 1965, p.113.
2. Van Wing 1930, p.418.

I have shown you the animals of the feast,
And I have brought you no other presents
Except palm wine,
That you may favour the procreation of [human] wealth.
And here are the kola nuts I brought for you.

33 / Fecundity and Immortality[1]

This prayer from the Central Luo of Uganda was recited after the
cooking and offering of a sacrifice. The morsels of food were thrown
into the spirit hut by the son of one of the ancestors invoked in the
prayer, Lalwak. The dominant idea is that the birth of children ensures
hat the ancestors' names are not forgotten.

> Great men of Cua,
> You Lalwak, you Apille, you Keny, you Olango,
> Your food is here,
> Let the children have good health,
> The women have childbirth,
> So that your names may not be obliterated.

3. EARTH, THE FERTILE MOTHER
OF LIVING THINGS

Introduction

The eleven prayers in this section illustrate the theme of earth as
mother of living things, children, cattle and crops. The earth is more
frequently worshipped as a deity in West Africa, but the soil can be
hailed in prayer as the source of food and prosperity, the support of
men in life and death, as well as a personalized goddess. For the
theistic Bushman, the earth is a symbol inseparable from the experience

---

1. Okot p'Bitek 1971, pp.97–8.

of God. For the Ibo and Yoruba the earth is personalized among the other deities known to them. Among other peoples, the earth receives no worship but is a potent symbol of life. In some of the prayers in this section there is no explicit mention of the earth, but analogy is made by those with a cattle culture between the children of men and of cattle, and by those who practice agriculture between children and crops. The life cycles of men, animals and crops are linked in the thought of African peoples, forming a single, harmonious movement.

34 | May We Bear Children and Cattle[1]

The prophet-leader of the Meru of Kenya, the Mugwe, made this prayer during a drought. The prayer was offered after a sacrificial sheep had led the worshippers to a pool of water in a sacred grove. The prayer, which followed the sacrifice, asks for children and cattle and for the protection of both. God is addressed as Murungu.

> Murungu, we pray, help us,
> That we may live, have strength,
> May we bear children and cattle.
> And those who have them,
> They too say:
> Help our children.

35 | A Blessing and a Curse[2]

This elaborate invocation was made by an elder of the Kithuri clan among the Meru of Kenya. Besides praying for the multiplication of boys and girls, goats and cattle, he calls down a curse on those who hate and those who 'do wrong'. In their turn, they are cursed with the 'curse of the back'. This refers to a vulgar gesture made by women who show their anus to an adversary in contempt.

1. Bernardi 1959, p.114.
2. Bernardi 1959, pp.121–2.

May people be well, may they be well,
Male, female, male, female,
Goats, cattle, boys and girls;
May they multiply themselves.
Bad luck go away from us.
The [uncircumcised] man who hates another,
May he perish.
Who hates these people of mine,
May he perish.
The man who does wrong,
May he also perish.
The man who curses another,
Who says: 'May he perish',
He will die on the spot,
Cursed with the curse of the back.

36 | To The Hill Deity Who Gave Me Birth[1]

This prayer is used by the priest of Okpuje in the land of the Ibo,
Nigeria. It accompanies an offering of kola-nuts, food and chickens,
held skywards. Besides asking for food and offspring, the prayer asks a
blessing on all men. Ezechitoke is the Earth Deity; Ogwuokpuje is the
Hill Deity.

Ezechitoke, Earth Deity,
Ugwuokpuje that gave me birth,
Give me things to eat;
Give me offspring;
Give me wives;
Give me money;
Bless all men.

1. Ezeanya in Dickson and Ellingworth 1969, p.39.

At a hand-washing ceremony which is part of the ritual celebrating the birth of a child, the Ibo of Nigeria pray for the fertility of crops and children. The refrain: 'Earth Goddess, hear' is repeated by all present, beating their hands lightly on the earth.

> Fellow men, we shall all live,
> Earth Goddess, hear.
> Whoever plants, let him dig up and eat.
> Earth Goddess, hear.
> We shall give birth to sons.
> Earth Goddess, hear.
> We shall give birth to daughters.
> Earth Goddess, hear.
> We shall train them.
> Earth Goddess, hear.
> When we are old they will feed us.
> Earth Goddess, hear.
> Whoever sees us with an evil eye,
> When he plants may the floods sweep his mounds away.
> Whoever wishes us evil,
> May he break his fist on the ground.
> We are broody hens, we have chicks.
> We do not fly up,
> We look after our brood.
> We do not eye others with an evil eye.
> This big-headed thing [child] that came home yesterday,
> He is yet a seed.
> If you wish that he germinates
> And grows to be a tree,
> We shall be ever thankful.
> Earth Goddess, hear;
> He will grow to be like his stock.

1.   Agunwa 1967, p.101.

38 / O Mother, Deliver Us[1]

In Adõ, a Yoruba town in Nigeria, Odúdúwà, an agent of creation, is venerated as a goddess. In other places this person is said to have lived as a man. In either case, he or his female Divinity was a rival to the Yoruba Creator-deity Orìsá-Nlà. The name means 'Chief who created being'.

> O Mother, we beseech thee to deliver us;
> Look after us,
> Look after [our] children;
> Thou who art established at Adó.

39 / Earth, I Depend Upon You[2]

Although Earth has no priests or priestesses among the Ashanti of Ghana, people make offerings to her for the fertility of their crops. This Ashanti drum poem expresses human dependence on Earth.

> Earth, condolences,
> Earth, condolences,
> Earth and dust,
> The dependable one,
> I lean upon you.
> Earth, when I am about to die,
> I lean upon you.
> Earth, while I am alive,
> I depend upon you.
> Earth, while I am alive,
> I depend upon you.
> Earth that receives dead bodies,
> The Creator's drummer says:
> From wherever he went,
> He has roused himself,
> He has roused himself.

1. Idowu 1962, p.27.
2. Busia 1954, p.195.

40 / The Forgotten God[1]

This is a very common chant at the New Year festival of the Ga of Ghana. It is a prayer for an abundance of the fruits of the earth, animals for meat, water to drink and crops for food. Bleku, the deity mentioned in the hymn, is now unknown. Only his name is remembered.

> Exalted! Exalted! Exalted!
> Ho, Priestly people!
> Let Bleku give peace.
> Meat, meat,
> Water, water,
> Let blessings bless
> Masses of food.

41 / Prayer of the New Year Festival[2]

This prayer is recited by the Ga of Ghana at their New Year festival. It accompanies the first fruits libation of corn-wine. The priest raises the calabash to his lips, but does not drink. Instead he pours a libation out upon the earth and then prays for continued prosperity in hunting and harvest.

> Hail, hail, hail.
> May happiness come.
> May meat come,
> May corn come.
> Just as the farmers work
> And look forward to the reaping,
> So may we sit again as we are sitting now.
> May our enemies turn from us and go . . .
> Lord return.

1. Field 1937, p.13.
2. Field 1937, p.55.

42 / Prayer of the Gunnu Ritual[1]

The Gunnu ritual of the Nupe in Nigeria is the cult of God, rather than of ancestral and other spirits. The Etsu Dazi mentioned is the chief and the prayer for health and food is said after beer has been poured out upon the earth and before everyone partakes of the beer that is left over. Although made by men, Gunnu has an autonomy of its own.

> Lord God, take this.
> The Etsu Dazi ordered us to make Gunnu.
> Gunnu, may the town have health.
> The food of the soil,
> May it thrive greatly.
> The women, God give them children.
> May the town have health.
> Rain may fall,
> Yam may thrive,
> Corn may thrive.
> God may cause that everything shall prosper.

43 / Prayer of the Tsoede Ritual[2]

In Mokwa village of the Nupe, Nigeria, The Sheshi, or priest-king-maker, lays his insignia, the chain of Tsoede, on the ground, within a sacred grove. After an offering of a chicken and beer, he prays for prosperity.

> God, we have come.
> God, everybody has come.
> This ancient thing of Tsoede
> Which is lying on the ground,
> It says we should bring beer.
> Because of the old saying
> Which we have heard,

---

1. Nadel 1954, p.81.
2. Nadel 1942, p.141.

Because of that, we bring beer and a fowl.

Tsoede, make the whole town prosper.

44 | *Prayer for the Maturity of Girls and Crops*[1]

This Acholi prayer from the Central Luo of Uganda is addressed to
the territorial spirit or chiefdom Jok, venerated at the twin shrines of
Baka and Alela. It is recited after morsels of millet bread, goat's
meat, chicken and *oribi* have been thrown into the caves of the shrine.

> Jok of our chiefdom,
> Jok of our forefathers,
> We have brought food for you.
> We have brought chicken and goat.
> We have brought termite and butter.
> Our insides are clean;
> We have brought you food with clean insides,
> Eat it.
> We have brought your children,
> Here they are.
> We beseech you, Oh!
> Let your children have childbirth.
> Untie the young women
> So that childbirth may fall on them.
> The little girls are here,
> Let them develop breasts.
> You, Jok of our chiefdom,
> Let the crops yield,
> The rains fall peacefully.
> Let the children have good health.
> The sicknesses that are coming,
> Let them pass far away.

---

1.   Okot p'Bitek 1971, p.69

4. HEALTH AND HEALING

Introduction

Health and healing are most important values in African traditional religion, connected as they are with the fundamental theme of life. Sickness, for the African, is a diminution of life, a threat posed to life, and healing is an activity second only to that of giving life. Petition for healing is probably the most common subject of prayer, as texts classified in other sections besides make clear. With the exception of the Nyakyusa prayer from Tanzania, all the texts collected in this section are addressed to the Supreme Being. In the case of the Ibo from Nigeria and the Luguru from Tanzania, prayer is addressed to other divinities or spirits besides the Supreme Being himself. And for the Luyia of Kenya, an almost dualistic belief is presupposed in the text, in which the 'white god' is asked to drive away the 'black god', the latter being an independent, if weaker, force to whom all evil and sickness is ascribed.

The prayers which derive from a characteristically theistic tradition seem to express a high level of confidence and intimacy. For the Nuer of Sudan, God is 'friend . . . in this village' while for their neighbours, the Dinka, God joins in the evil which befalls mankind, showing concern, and struggling with man against it. Both the Meru of Kenya and the Anuak of Sudan express the feeling that, in turning to the Creator, they are taking the only course of action possible. There is no one else to whom to turn. On the other hand, both the Meru and the Luguru of Tanzania—the latter placing greater emphasis on ancestral beliefs—clearly indicate that prayer for the sick must be accompanied by medical treatment, and this is assumed by the Dinka of Sudan as well. Lastly, in the Aladura prayer from West Africa, we have a typical example from an African independent church, proverbially pre-occupied with healing from a complex of sin, sickness and sorcery. Healing is the principal aim of such churches. 'There are many blind to cure, there are many deaf to hear.'

45 | *Overcome All These Troubles*[1]

In this text, a Meru medicine-man from Kenya prays for the cure of a sick man he is treating. He addresses God as Nyaga (brightness),

1. Bernardi 1959, p.129.

and confesses that he does not know any other form of prayer. He begs for the mercy of God, Murungu.

> Nyaga help his man that he may be well,
> That he may recover tomorrow,
> And may you want to help this man to be well;
> And, as overcoming you overcame,
> Overcome all these troubles,
> And have mercy on me,
> Because we do not know how to pray to Murungu,
> [Differently] from what we say now.

46 | *Friend, God, We Tell You About This Wound*[1]

This prayer was said by a man of the Nuer of Sudan, representing the home party of a youth injured in a fight with a man of the next village. After the attackers had offered sacrifice, it was the turn of the home party to immolate a castrated ram. It was consecrated by rubbing ashes on its back and a libation of water was poured over its tethering peg, before the prayer was made. This was the 'ransom'. The worshipper addresses Kwoth, God.

> Friend, God, who is in this village
> As you are very great,
> We tell you about this wound,
> For you are the God of our home in very truth.
> We tell you about the fight of this lad,
> Let the wound heal,
> Let it be ransomed.

47 | *You Are Called to Join With Them In The Evil*[2]

This was the final invocation in a Dinka sacrifice from the Sudan before the sacrificial calf was thrown. The prayer is for a cure from illness caused by witchcraft, and is addressed mainly to Divinity himself

---

1. Evans-Pritchard 1956, p.112.
2. Lienhardt 1961, p.230.

who enters into men's conflicts and problems. Other divinities, and even the illness itself are addressed, particular expressions of the human encounter with the divine.

> You Earth, you are called by my words,
> And you, Divinity, you are called by my words,
> Because you look after all people, and are greater than anyone,
> And, if evil has befallen them,
> Then you are called to come and join with them in it also.
> And you are not now called for good, you are called for evil.
> Come, help!
> O You Flesh, divinity of Pagong,
> If you are called, then you will indeed hear me,
> And you Awar grass, you will hear.
> And you Flesh of my father and Fig-tree of my father,
> And Head-carrying ring of my father, you will hear.
> O Power [illness], we have separated you from ourselves,
> Release him
> We have given you the bull Mayan,
> Release him indeed!

48 / Prayer Against Fever And Illness[1]

This invocation was made by the Dinka of Sudan, not on any specific occasion, but as a general supplication for good health. It is addressed to Divinity throughout and accompanies a sacrifice.

> You Divinity, we shall kill your ox,
> And better that you should be pleased with us.
> You will let us walk in health,

1. Lienhardt 1961, pp.231–2.

And we have made a feast so that there should be no fever,

And that no other illness should seize people,

That they may all be well.

And if my clansman travels,

Then let him complete his journey without sickness,

And let no evil befall him or anybody.

And you Divinity, do not bring evil upon us,

And I shall be pleased.

You women, clap your hands and sing.

And *wuu* away the fever, that nothing may be wrong with us.

You tribe of my father, walk in health,

Nothing shall harm us,

And Divinity will be pleased with us,

And we will pray to Divinity that there may be no bad things,

And sing . . .

49 | *Thou Art The Only One*[1]

This prayer on behalf of a sick child was made by the Anuak of Sudan.
It is addressed to the Creator as 'the only one' who can help. God is
great and there is no other.

> O God, thou art great,
>
> Thou art the one who created me,
>
> I have no other.
>
> God, thou art in the heavens,
>
> Thou art the only one:
>
> Now my child is sick,
>
> And thou wilt grant me my desire.

50 | *Drive Away The Black God*[2]

For the Luyia of Kenya, besides the Creator, Wele—also called
Khakaba (provider) and Ratsari (white)—there is also an independent,

1. Seligman 1932, p.519.
2. Wagner 1954, p.44.

if weaker, personal source of evil, Wele Gumali (black god). This prayer is for a sick man, 'your person', and it asks Wele to drive away the black god.

> Wele, you who made us walk in your country,
> You who made the cattle and the things which are in it,
> You may spit the medicine on your person,
> He may recover and walk well,
> He may plant his gardens.
> Drive away the black god,
> He may leave your person,
> He may move into the snake
> And into the abandoned homestead;
> He may leave our house.

51 | *May You Spit Upon Us The Medicine*[1]

This short Luyia ejaculation from Kenya asks Wele, God, to 'spit medicine' upon mankind. God's medicine includes good health, fertility, increase of life and of possessions. The prayer is said at dawn.

> Po! God, may the day dawn well;
> May you spit upon us the medicine
> So that we may walk well!

52 | *May We Not Be Tormented With Maladies*[2]

In this Ibo prayer from Nigeria against sickness and death, the Supreme Being is invoked before the minor god, Agbala, and other spirits.

---

1. Wagner 1949, p.170.
2. Ezeanya 1969, p.38.

God and the spirits are invited to eat kola-nut—an extension of a human courtesy to the spirit world.

> God, eat kola-nut,
> Spirits, eat kola-nut,
> Sky, eat kola-nut,
> Agbala, eat kola-nut.
> May we not die,
> May we not perish,
> May we not be sick,
> May we not be tormented with maladies.

53 | May Sickness Be Slight[1]

This ritual formula from the Nyakyusa of Tanzania is addressed to the spirits of the hereditary priests of Lubaga. It accompanies a libation of milk and asks for various favours connected with health and prosperity.

> Here is your milk . . . .
> May the locusts pass,
> May sickness be slight,
> May milk be plentiful,
> May the cows calve!

54 | Help Us Through These Roots[2]

In this prayer, the Luguru of Tanzania address both God and the ancestral spirits, asking them to cure a sickness. If the sickness has a

1. Wilson 1959, p.32.
2. Mawinza 1968, p.45.

human cause, they ask that their medicinal roots be effective as a remedy. The prayer is concluded by spitting water towards the four cardinal points—a confession rite. *Kutzimu* is the dwelling-place of the spirits of the departed.

> You, Father God,
> Who are in the heavens and below;
> Creator of everything, and omniscient
> [Of] how the earth and the heavens [were made].
> We are but little children
> Unknowing anything evil;
> If this sickness has been brought by man,
> We beseech thee, help us through these roots!
> In case it is inflicted by you, the Conserver,
> Likewise do we entreat your mercy on your child;
> Also you, our grandparents who sleep in *kutzimu*,
> We entreat all of you, sleep on one side.
> All ancestors, male and females, great and small,
> Help us in this trouble, have compassion on us;
> So that we can also sleep peacefully,
> And hither do I spit out this mouthful of water!
> Pu-pu! Pu-pu!
> Please listen to our earnest request!

55 / Go And Loose The Captives' Fetters[1]

This hymn is used during the ordination ceremony in the Aladura Church of West Africa. The ordinand is commissioned to go and heal people from sin and sickness, a major preoccupation of the church. God is called by strange, esoteric names, peculiar to the Aladura.

---

1.   Turner 1967, p.266.

Listen ye not to the mockers,
Ajajgogriea, he sends you.
Go and loose the captives' fetters,
Ajajbieurar, he sends you.
There are many blind to cure,
There are many deaf to hear,
Who are waiting Saviour Christ,
And the time is passing by.

5. MEMORIAL

Introduction

The approach adopted by scholars towards traditional religious
systems in Africa has often been static and ahistorical. In face of the
mounting evidence collected by oral historians, such an approach is
no longer tenable. There are a number of prayers in other sections of
this book which are attributed to historical personalities or which
celebrate historic events. This short section gathers together eight
texts in which there is a direct appeal to the past associated with the
efficacy of the prayer itself. African traditional religions may not be
historical, in the sense that they are typically focused on specific,
historical events, or that their adepts have a highly developed historical
sense, but history plays its part in African religious consciousness, and
the historical study of African religion is eminently possible. Moreover,
as these prayers show, the idea of memorial, or continuity with the
past providing an understanding of the present and a hope for the
future, is a value which African religion shares with the so-called
'historical' religions of Judaism, Christianity and Islam.

The three prayers from the Kikuyu of Kenya stress the necessity of
the worshipper being in harmony with his ancestors, by worshipping
God in the very manner in which his ancestors worshipped him, so
that God will be with the living in their turn. The Dinka of Sudan have
a very strong consciousness of their ancestors praying with them and of
their prayer being a prayer 'of the long distant past, prayer of my
ancestors'.

The Nyoro of Uganda and the Edo of Nigeria pray to, rather than with, their forefathers, but they desire the success and comfort that is associated with the latter, and beg them to do as they have been done by. Finally, the prayers of the Zulu Zionists or Nazarites in South Africa celebrate the re-creation of the Biblical holy places in their own land, and see in them a foretaste of heaven itself.

56 | Blessing for a New Homestead[1]

This Kikuyu prayer from Kenya asks a blessing on a new homestead. God is addressed as the 'Great Elder' dwelling on Kere-Nyaga[2] the 'shining mount' Kenya, symbol of his transcendence and absolute sway. The worshippers are 'in harmony' with their ancestors. The prayer was recited after a libation of beer or milk had been poured from a horn over the foundations of the new house, and with the presiding elder raising the horn towards the mountain.

> You, the Great Elder, who dwells on the Kere-Nyaga,
> Your blessing allows homesteads to spread.
> Your anger destroys homesteads.
> We beseech you, and in this we are in harmony
> With the spirits of our ancestors;
> We ask you to guard this homestead and let it spread.
> Let the women, herd and flock be prolific.

> *Chorus*
> *Peace, praise ye Ngai [God],*
> *Peace be with us!*

57 | Prayer for Rain under God's Tree[3]

This prayer was made by the Kikuyu of Kenya before the sacrifice of a lamb and before the spraying and sprinkling of milk and honey-

---

1. Kenyatta 1938, pp.81–2.
2. This name is transcribed variously in Kikuyu and Meru texts: Kirinyaga, Kerinyaga, Kere-Nyaga, but the accepted orthography is Kirinyaga in Kikuyu nowadays.
3. Kenyatta 1938, p.247.

beer in a libation for rain. The worship was conducted under a Mugumo tree, a specially large ritual tree, known as 'God's tree'. God is addressed as Ngai, the Creator or Sky God, but also as Mwene Nyaga (possessor of brightness). He lives on Kere-Nyaga, the 'mountain of brightness'. Because God heard their ancestors under this tree, the elders trust God will hear them also.

Reverend Elder [God] who lives on Kere-Nyaga,

You who make mountains tremble and rivers flood;

We offer to you this sacrifice that you may bring us rain.

People and children are crying;

Sheep, goats and cattle are crying.

Mwene Nyaga, we beseech you,

With the blood and fat of this lamb we are going sacrifice to you.

Refined honey and milk we have brought for you.

We praise you in the same way as our forefathers used to praise you,

Under this very same tree,

And you heard them and brought them rain.

We beseech you to accept this, our sacrifice,

    And bring us rain of prosperity.

Response
Peace, we beseech you,
Ngai, peace be with us!

58 / We Know That You Are With Us[1]

This is a prayer of the Watu wa Mungu, the 'People of God', an independent religious sect among the Kikuyu of Kenya, which broke away from the Church of Scotland Mission. They believe that Mwene Nyaga, (possessor of brightness), the Kikuyu God, has given them

---

1. Kenyatta 1938, p.278.

prophetical power. They are *arathi* or seers. God is addressed also as Ngai, and the prayer expresses confidence in him. He is with them as he was with their ancient ancestors.

> O Lord, your power is greater than all powers.
> Under your leadership we cannot fear anything.
> It is you who has given us prophetical power,
> And has enabled us to foresee and interpret everything.
> We beseech you to protect us in all trials and torments.
> We know that you are with us,
> Just as you were with our ancient ancestors,
> Under your protection there is nothing that we cannot
> overcome.
> Peace, praise ye Ngai,
> Peace, peace, peace be with us!

59 | *Prayer of My Ancestors, You are Spoken Now*[1]

This invocation by the Dinka of the Sudan accompanied a sacrifice offered for the cure of a sick man. The sacrificial beast was a grey-coloured ox (*malith*) which was expected to urinate as a sign of divine favour. The ancestors join the worshippers in the sacrifice, for the words being used now are taken from an ancient prayer, the prayer of a prominent ancestor, Guejok.

> And you of my father, if you are called, then you will help me.
> And join yourself with my words.
> And I did not speak that my children should become ill;
> That quarrel is an old matter.
> And you, *malith*, even though you have not urinated,
> You urinated on the way, when you were being brought here.

---

1. Lienhardt 1961, p.221.

And you, my prayer, and you prayer of the long distant past,
Prayer of my ancestors, you are spoken now.
Meet together, ee!
It is that of my ancestor Guejok,
It is not of the tongue only,
It is that of Guejok,
It is not of the tongue only.

60 | *Prayer for Entering a New House*[1]

This prayer of the Nyoro of Uganda is addressed to the spirits of the
ancestors who are thought to enter a newly built house and to dwell
there as guardians. The owner of the house throws millet and simsim
seeds as an offering, and then he and his wife also eat some. In the
prayer he sees his own house-building as part of a tradition begun
by his forefathers.

My father built,
And his father built,
And I have built.
Leave me to live here in success,
Let me sleep in comfort,
And have children.
There is food for you.

61 | *Unceasing Guardians of the Living*[2]

This prayer was recited by a senior man and woman of the lineage
among the Edo of Benin Kingdom, Nigeria. The occasion was the burial
of a dead man, seen by the Edo as his 'planting' or transformation into
a guardian spirit of the family. The senior son and the children threw
chalk and cowries into the grave after the prayer.

---

1. Roscoe 1923, p.213.
2. Fortes and Dieterlen 1965, p. 105.

Your children whom you have left here,
You should order money for them.
You should send them children.
You should send them everything
That is used for living in the world . . .
As they have lived to do this for you,
Let their children live to do it for them . . .
As you looked after your children
When you were in the world,
So you should look after them unceasingly.

62 / A Foretaste of Heaven[1]

In this hymn the Zulu adepts of the Nazarite or Zionist Church
remember with joy Ekuphakameni, the village of their prophet. The
name literally means a 'high and elevated place' and to go there is to
obtain a foretaste of heaven, for its water is a spring of living water
that lasts for ever.

I remember Ekuphakameni,
Where there is gathered
The Holy Church
Of the Nazarites.

I remember Ekuphakameni,
Where the springs are,
Springs of living water,
Lasting for ever.

I remember Ekuphakameni;
A loudly falling cascade
Is the response of the Saints
Of the Nazarites.

1. Sundkler 1948, p.292.

Ye all who thirst
Come ye to Ekuphakameni;
Ye will drink freely
From the springs of water.

63 | Dream Visit to the Holy Place[1]

This hymn of the Zulu Nazarites or Zionists of South Africa is believed
to have been revealed to a woman medium in a vision, during which
she paid a dream visit to the prophet's village where she met the risen
prophet, Isaiah Shembe. The village is called the 'holy city' and the
prophet is given divine status as 'Star of Heaven', and even as Jehovah
himself. Dingaan was a former Zulu Chief.

> The spring time of the earth has come;
> The time is here.
> Be afraid, you hartebeestes,
> You are recalled to Ekuphakameni.
>
> The Star of Heaven
> Rose in the East
> Until it entered
> Into the holy city.
>
> Let your testimony echo widely.
> There he is, Jehovah.
> Now he has come,
> You people of Dingaan.

6. MEDIATION AND RECIPROCITY

Introduction

Eight texts are grouped here to illustrate a theme that certainly coexists
with many of the themes in other sections of this book, particularly

1. Sundkler 1948, pp. 284–5.

73

with memorial, the theme treated in the preceding section. Mediation and reciprocity are two aspects of human relations with ancestral spirits, and it follows that they will be especially verified in those religious systems where ancestors occupy an important, if not the central, position. For the Nyakyusa of Tanzania, the Ngoni of Malawi and the Central Luo of Uganda, the relationship between the ancestors and Supreme Deity is in some way equivocal. Prayer is directed to heroes and eminent ancestors, and relationship with them receives attention that is almost exclusive of any other considerations. The Nyakyusa examples show very clearly that the duties of the living and the dead are reciprocal: the dead must look after the living, both morally and materially, and the living must remember the dead and offer them worship and keep faith with them. The veneration which the Ngoni have for their eminent ancestors is founded in their own aristocratic tradition. All real power lies on the side of the ancestors; what is demanded of the living is an attitude of complete abandonment. For the Central Luo the ancestors are the source of life and health, but they, in their turn, need 'to be fed' by their living descendants with regular sacrifices and offerings.

Mediation is of greater importance among the Mende of Sierra Leone and prayer is to God through the ancestors, who are in his 'arms'. This is, perhaps, implied for the Safwa of Tanzania also, who expose their problems at a common feast to which the ancestors are invited almost as equals.

64 / Receive Our Fellow Who Has Died[1]

This short, ejaculatory prayer by Mwasalemba, a Nyakyusa from Tanzania, is addressed to the shade of a senior relative or ancestor. The worshipper offers and shares beans with the shade to appease him after the death of a kinsman caused by the shade 'brooding over him'. Death is a punishment for neglecting to offer sacrifice to the shades.

> You shade!
> We are eating these beans.

1. Wilson 1957, p.70.

Since you have brooded over our fellow
Who has died,
Receive him.

65 | *Because There is Hunger, You Caused Theft*[1]

This Nyakyusa prayer from Tanzania is addressed to their heroes or
senior ancestors, among whom Kyala—now identified as the Christian
God—was traditionally neither separate nor supreme. The heroes
created the crops and the animals. If they want men to avoid theft,
it is in their interest to give them food. The prayer accompanies a
sacrifice and the burying of the sacrificial meat.

Here is your cow, your food.
We pray to Kyala. May theft go away.
Give us food and beans and millet,
May we eat and be satisfied . . .
It is said that the sweet potatoes are scarce now, help us.
You Mwakabule, Mwakomo . . . . This is your cow, Mwaijonga.
This is your meat.
I shall seek another also which we shall give you like this.
May the locusts go away.
It is you who have caused theft because there is hunger.
At night, since we eat scraps of food our bellies are disquieted . . . .
May we be satisfied.
People are eating millet porridge;
When food is plentiful they say it's horrible.
When someone eats millet porridge he dies, it kills a man.
We pray to him, this Kyala, because we do not know him,
So we say: "You Mwaijonga drive away the hunger.
Give all of us, Mwaipopo's people, food
And hear us all."

---

1.   Wilson 1959, p.77.

66 / We Can Only Speak Your Names[1]

This Ngoni prayer from Malawi mentions their eminent ancestors
by name and is an example of complete abandonment to the will of
the powers that rule the world. It is offered here for a sick child. The
worshippers want her recovery, but it is the affair of the ancestors
to cure her if they wish. Prayer accompanies sacrifice.

> O thou Gumede!
> O thou Mputa!
> O thou great chief!
> Here is your beast.
> That your child may be healed,
> Look on what is yours.
> May you remain well
> And your child recover.
> We do not know,
> We do not know,
> If you say that she will die,
> She is yours, this child of yours.
> It is your affair.
> As for us, we long that your child may recover.
> If she dies, this child of yours,
> We can only speak your names.
> We cry to you for her.

67 / We Are Your People[2]

This text from the Ngoni of Malawi expresses sorrow and puzzlement
at the continued refusal of the ancestors, especially the old Paramount
Chief, to grant a petition on behalf of their children. 'Why do you
refuse us?' 'We . . . are your people.'

1. Read 1956, p.198.
2. Read 1956, p. 199

Alas, O Paramount,
Alas, O Father,
Why do you refuse us?
What do you say about your child?
We say we are your people,
Alas, O Paramount.

68 / Our Forefathers Who Are in Your Arms[1]

Among the Mende of Sierra Leone, God (Ngewo) is approached
through the ancestors, just as a living chief is approached through
intermediaries. In this prayer a petition is offered to God through Kenei
Momo and Nduawo, particular ancestors remembered by the worshipper.

O God, let it reach to Kenei Momo,
Let it reach to Nduawo,
Let it reach to all our forefathers
Who are in your arms.

69 / We Are Here in Your Compound[2]

There is a certain familiarity and irreverence about the way the
Safwa of Tanzania address their ancestors in this prayer. The
'compound' is the burial-place, although the worshippers know that
ancestors are in 'the white place', the spirit realm. A feast is prepared, a
libation of beer poured on the grave, and an offering of millet flour
and a chicken drowned in beer and roasted. The prayer is a summons
to the feast.

Hey you people!
Wake up in your home, if you are there.

---

1. Harris 1950, p.201.
2. Harwood, 1970, p.36.

Hey, Ndele, drink this beer!
You people, if you are there in this compound,
Take this beer.
Mlangali, drink this beer at your compound.
Nkalanga, beer!
Mwagamba, you too, if you are here.
You who are in the white place,
We are here in your compound.
We are disappearing because of disease.
We have come here, you people!

70 | Why Should We Be Afraid Of You?[1]

Before immolating a goat at the ceremony of dedicating a shrine to
his father, Lakwor son of Lalwak, of the Ugandan Central Luo,
invokes all of the ancestors, confident that his offering is accepted
and that there is nothing to fear.

> Ancestors, you have accepted the food
> We offered you today.
> Here is the food.
> Why should we be afraid of you?
> Your billy-goat is here today.
> Today, drink its blood.
> Fiends that are coming
> Let them pass away.

71 | If We Were Not Present Who Would Feed You?[2]

This prayer accompanies the sacrifice of a chicken at a shrine of the
Central Luo, Uganda. The worshipper asks that there be no death,
arguing that, if he and his fellows were not alive, there would be no one
to 'feed' the ancestors with offerings.

---

1. Okot p'Bitek 1971, p.97.
2. Okot p'Bitek 1971, p.98.

Our fathers,
Your chicken is here.
Let us have good health.
Let there be no death in the homes.
If we were not present,
Who would feed you?

7. GRATITUDE, A FOUNDATION FOR TRUST

Introduction

Prayer is very far from being merely a crisis measure in the religious traditions of Africa, a means of comprehending and confronting events which are beyond man's control. The eight prayers of thanksgiving in this section demonstrate this clearly. In his own achievements, in his very prosperity and success, the African is aware of the divine presence. Furthermore, he understands that the best way of showing gratitude is through continued fidelity in action. This is explicit in the Kikuyu text. However, gratitude is a foundation for trust also. If a man has experienced divine favour in the past, his gratefulness is also an act of faith in the continuation of that favour. Finally, gratitude is an aspect of the praise offered to the powers that govern his life in the world.

In religions with a marked theistic emphasis, God's presence and favour are overwhelming. All is his, as the first of the Pygmy texts demonstrates. In the Kikuyu and the second Pygmy texts, the worshipper expresses the impossibility of ever showing sufficient gratitude to God. The example from the Galla of Ethiopia clearly shows how gratitude develops into trust for the immediate future and the two prayers from Ghana combine both ideas.

Although mediation is a factor in both the religion of the Kamba of Kenya and the Luba of Zaïre, both their texts in this section are addressed to the Creator, but it is interesting to note that no requests are voiced. These are prayers of pure praise and thanksgiving. The final text is from the Alur of Uganda, one of the Central Luo groups. It is a prayer of first-fruits at harvest time, addressed to a territorial spirit, and, in spite of its divinatory character, is an expression of thanksgiving without an explicit petition.

72 / I Am Your Warrior[1]

This prayer is attributed to Gikuyu, the legendary founder of the
Kikuyu people in Kenya. After God (the Great Elder) has shown him
the fertile land of the Kikuyu, the ancestor utters this prayer of praise
and gratitude, translating his thanksgiving into active readiness to do
God's will and be his 'warrior'.

> O My Father, Great Elder,
> I have no words to thank you,
> But with your deep wisdom
> I am sure that you can see
> How I value your glorious gifts.
> O My Father, when I look upon your greatness,
> I am confounded with awe.
> O Great Elder,
> Ruler of all things earthly and heavenly,
> I am your warrior,
> Ready to act in accordance with your will.

73 / You Have Given Me All[2]

This thank-offering for first fruits comes from the Pygmies of Zaïre.
God is owner of all and he shares all with man. Man can only praise
him and return to him what is his. Nothing is requested in this prayer.

> O God, you have formed heaven and earth;
> You have given me all the goods that the earth bears!
> Here is your part, my God.
> Take it!

1. Kenyatta 1966, p.3.
2. Nyom 1964, p.421.

74 / *Thanksgiving For the Birth of a Child*[1]

In this text the Pygmies of Zaïre celebrate the birth of a child and offer it to God in thanksgiving, together with food that God has given them. God is a firm support, like a termite heap, and nothing man can offer is worthy of him.

> O God, thanks!
> Here is the human being whom you gave us.
> Today we bring you the food that you have given us,
> You, my termite heap on which I lean,
> From which come the termites that I eat.
> Lord we thank you; you have given us joy
> With the numerous births you have given us.
> Nothing of all that we offer you is worthy of you.

75 / *Never Can We Thank You For Your Deeds*[2]

This Ashanti prayer from Ghana is addressed to God (Odomankoma), 'full of mercy', and it accompanies a thanksgiving feast to which the lesser deities are invited. The favour for which the worshippers are grateful makes them bold to ask for fertility and health. Brenhoma is a village in the story of which this scene is a part.

> The year has come round, great Odomankoma,
> Never can we thank you for your deeds and blessing for us.
> Tano Kofi and all the seventy-seven gods of Brenhoma,.
> Come now and eat from our hands and bless your people.
> Let all who are ill get well.
> Let all who are barren bear children.
> Let all who are impotent find remedy.
> Don't let them go blind or paralysed.
> We all beseech happiness,
> Let us have it.

---

1. Moreau 1960, p.548.
2. Konadu 1967, p.56.

The Ghanaian fisherman at the sea coast gives thanks to God for the blessings of the sea. God's favour makes him confident that he can overcome his own weakness. The prayer is influenced by Christian ideas and language.

Lord,
I sing your praise,
The whole day through until the night.
Dad's nets are filled,
I have helped him.
We have drawn them in,
Stamping the rhythm with our feet,
The muscles tense.
We have sung your praise.
On the beach, there were our mammies,
Who bought the blessing out of the nets,
Out of the nets into their basins.
They rushed to the market,
Returned and bought again.
Lord, what a blessing is the sea
With fish in plenty.
Lord, that is the story of your grace.
Nets tear, and we succumb
Because we cannot hold them.
Lord, with your praise we drop off to sleep.
Carry us through the night,
Make us fresh for the morning.
Hallelujah for the day!
And blessing for the night!
Amen.

---

1. Pawelzik 1968, p.24.

77 | Feeder Who Brings Me Up[1]

This Luba worshipper from Kasai, Zaïre, abandons himself in thanksgiving to God, his Father. After work, he brings an offering which he
describes as 'the small part of a dog'—the small part which is not
worthy of God.

> O Father, feeder, who brings me up,
> I have worked the fields with all my strength;
> Now I bring you the small part of a dog.

78 | The Great Worth of a Newborn Child[2]

The Kamba worshipper from Kenya thanks the Creator (Muumbi)
with great simplicity, and without further request, for the great gift
of a newborn child.

> O Muumbi,
> Thou who hast created[3]
> All human beings,
> Thou hast conferred
> A great benefit on us[4]
> By bringing us this child.

79 | Divinatory Harvest Prayer[5]

Jok Rubanga, addressed in this Alur prayer from Uganda, is the
territorial spirit whose worship was carried across Lake Albert (now

1. Nyom 1964, p.131.
2. Lindblom 1920, p.207.
3. Prof. J. Mbiti translates the Kamba text: 'thou who dost all human beings
   create', Mbiti 1970 p.195.
4. Prof. J. Mbiti translates the Kamba text: 'thou hast on us a great worth
   conferred', Mbiti, ibid.
5. Okot p'Bitek 1971, p.118.

Mobutu) from Bunyoro. The worshippers offer a cow and the first
fruits of the harvest. The prayer is part of an Alur myth about the
founding of Jukoth chiefdom. The divinatory petition in the prayer
was answered by the earth shaking and causing the victim's death.

Today we come here, we bring you a cow
And all the first fruits of the harvest.
We carried you across the Lake,
We did not steal you from somebody;
Here is the cow we bring to you.
If it is acceptable to you,
Let the cow die here.
If it is not, if you refuse it,
Let the cow not die.

8. CONVERSION, FORGIVENESS
AND PURIFICATION

Introduction

These three related themes are illustrated here by seventeen texts
from thirteen different peoples. Symbols of sin and evil vary from one
ethnic group to another, and there are widely differing moral codes
reflecting different ideals and goals in social behaviour. In spite of this,
it is probably true to say that African peoples as a whole acknowledged
an essentially 'given' world order and that they understood sin not
only as a contradiction of that order, but as a greater or lesser offense
against its spirit-guardians, the Creator and the ancestors, or other
spiritual beings. Although the deliberately distorting, negative
symbolism of taboo was everywhere present, the taboos themselves
were not isolated from the system of world or social order as it was
conceived. On the contrary, they served to reinforce and underline it.
The effectiveness of taboos derives from the danger which they threaten,
but African consciousness of sin is far from being merely a fear of the
consequences of breaking a taboo. Sin is a state of isolation and enmity,
entailing as it does the breaking of relationships between men and the
spirit world and between man and man.

84

The admission of guilt and the promise of conversion and amendment is present in all the types of the religious system. It reaches its most spiritual expression, perhaps, in theistic belief. The Meru of Kenya can pray for the conversion of other men's hearts; the Dinka of the Sudan picture Divinity as 'heartbroken' over man's wrong-doing, and as judging between him and his enemy. They present a man who recognizes that his decline in fortune is due to sins of pride and greed, and for whom salvation is not merely the liberation from sin's consequences, but from sin itself. It is impossible to say, after reading these texts, that in African traditional religion there was no ethical relationship with God, no idea of God as judge, and no idea of spiritual salvation.

In other religious systems, in which the Supreme Being is not encountered so directly, admission of guilt may be less forthright. Self-questioning, the protestation of innocence, and particularly the negative or prudential confession are all extremely common. This type of approach can also spill over into the prayers of the independent churches with their Christian and Biblical orientation. This is no less true for traditional ideas of purification. The desire to be cleansed from defilement can appear somewhat materialistic, as in the Ibo example from Nigeria. Yet even here defilement 'comes out of a man' and is not simply contracted exteriorly. For the Aladura West African Church, as for other African Christian movements, cleansing is from a complex of sin, witchcraft or sorcery, material defilement and sickness.

African believers project their experience of evil on to external forces and causes, and, realistically perhaps, they give greater importance to human machinations than to spiritual personifications of evil, even if they credit wicked men with preternatural powers of witchcraft or superior techniques of sorcery. The Meru of Kenya are able to enlist God's help against 'bad' spirits, and the Luyia (also of Kenya), as we saw in the section on health and healing, envisage a dualism of white and black gods. In general, however, malevolent spirits are not purely, or even mainly, morally bad, and evil does not escape the overall control of the Supreme Being, who may be a personification of all human experience, good and evil.

The Meru medicine-man, M. Kamunde, asks in this prayer for strength that comes with food and possessions, but he asks also to be saved from 'bad' spirits who trouble his sleep. Ngai is the name for God among the Kenya Meru.

> Ngai, you created me
> And you gave me strength.
> Every little thing in its entirety
> Is of Ngai.
> Instil strength into me,
> Give me all things:
> Millet, sorghum, beans, goats and lambs.
> Guard me from going to any resting place
> With bad spirits,
> Because bad spirits are they
> Who trouble a sleeping man.

81 | Prayer for the Conversion of the Unfaithful[2]

The Mugwe, or prophet-leader of Imenti in Meru, Kenya, having given advice to a client, makes his own prayer that the advice will be followed, that his work will be successful and that those who do not trust him may be converted.

> Almighty God,
> Have mercy on me.
> May this child of mine
> See these things,

1. Bernardi 1959, p.124.
2. Bernardi 1959, p.117.

So that my work
May be seen by all men,
And also those who do not trust me,
May their infidelity change.

82 / *Divinity, Heartbroken Because of Man*[1]

An unclaimed fishing spear in the house of a sick old man is seen
by the Dinka worshipper as evidence of witchcraft. This invocation
before the throwing of the sacrificial calf addresses not only the clan-
divinity, 'head-carrying ring', who causes paralysis, but Divinity
himself, heartbroken at man's sins and the judge between him and his
enemy. The Dinka are a Nilotic people of the Sudan.

Repeat my words. Thus it is.
You, head-carrying ring of my father,
I call on you because you are the one
Who wastes the limbs,
And if I call upon you,
You will hear my words.
And you, O Divinity,
You are the great person whom all venerate,
And you do not repulse your people
If no one has given you offence.
And if a man has done wrong,
You will be heartbroken because of him,
And if a man has kept malice in his heart,
Then you will decide between him and his enemy,
Because it is you who are the father of all people.
And I will mention the witch,
Because he came to bewitch,

1. Lienhardt 1961, p.228.

And a man was left behind him, sick.
O you Divinity, if it be a child
Who brought the spear,
And nothing evil comes with it,
Then we have no quarrel with the child.
But if it be a witch,
Then may he get his deserts.
And though he be a very strong witch,
Yet will he be overcome
By the fishing-spear of my father.

83 / Contrition for Pride and Greed[1]

In this prayer recorded among the Dinka of Sudan, a man associates
his present misfortunes with his former sins of greed and self-
complacency. He made boasts and he slaughtered his *majok* (an ox with
pied markings), an animal which the Dinka regard as particularly
desirable. Now Golong, an injurious power, is causing plague among
his cattle, according to the verdict of Mayan, who is a diviner. Dr.
Lienhardt was unable to translate two lines of the text.

Children of the ants,
We have suffered from dryness.
Why, I am without cattle,
Why, I am without grain. . . .
That is what I ask, ee!
I am a man who boasted of himself.
I slaughtered in my greed my *majok* ox.
Children of Aghok, my father,
The children of the ants are forsaken.
My father, the Creator, indeed created men.
We honour our father,

---

1. Lienhardt 1961, p.243.

That he may look in upon us.
Mayan honours divinity.
Mayan, son of Deng, divines.
It is Golong which devours our cattle.

84 | How Have I Wronged You ?[1]

Mwaisumo, from the Nyakyusa of Tanzania, gives an account of a prayer when a child is ill with sores of the mouth. An oracle has divined that the shades are the cause. The prayer accompanies a rite of confession in which water is blown out of the mouth to signify getting rid of the sinful state. The worshipper is loath to admit he has done wrong. He asks a conditional forgiveness.

You Father, you N. . . . . ., you N. . . . . .,
Why are you angry, father?
Since you left me,
I have nourished the children.
How have I wronged you?
Even though I have wronged you,
Forgive me father.
May the child recover.
Stand by me.

85 | Avert this Evil[2]

The head of the Ibo family in Nigeria prays before the ancestral emblems asking that a sickness, the expected consequence of a heated quarrel, may be averted. The prayer is followed by the offering of a chicken and some yams. The ancestors are invited to break the ritual kola-nut with the living.

---

1. Wilson 1957, p.183
2. Agunwa 1967, pp.97–8.

All our forefathers, come and eat kola.
All those who gave us birth, come and hear.
Quell the quarrel,
Quell the hot exchange of words.
We are not the first to err,
Neither the last.
This is your white hen
And these are the yams.
The mistake has been made;
It will not happen again.
Aver this evil.
Avert this evil.
Avert this evil.
The invisible spirits that molest us,
Eat this and be appeased.

86 / *We Did Not Rob A Man To Build*[1]

Clement Agunwa's Ibo character from Nigeria, Mr. Nwakor, recites
this prayer after digging the foundations for his new house. He holds
a tethered goat by the rope in one hand, and the sacrificial knife in
the other. Those present touch the earth, before the goat is immolated.
Its blood is sprinkled on the foundations and its meat consumed by the
worshippers. The prayer, which is mainly directed at those who might
envy the building, begins with a negative, or prudential confession.

We did not rob a man to build.
We did not rob a man to build.
As we build, may we live in it till we are old.
When we follow our fathers.
May our children and their children live here.

1. Agunwa 1967, p.116.

Whoever is envious of us,
When he builds his own may it catch fire.
Whoever is not envious of us,
May he safely run in here for shelter
When he is caught by the rain.

87 | *Prayer For Purity*[1]

The Nigerian novelist Chinua Achebe puts this prayer into the mouth
of an Ibo woman at the Festival of the First Pumpkin Leaves. The
prayer, which is addressed to Ulu, (God), is a petition for purification
from defilement—defilement of speech, sight, hearing, touch and
kinship. The woman holds pumpkin leaves in her hand, believing that
the defilement will go when the priest snatches the leaves as he passes.

Great Ulu, who kills and saves,
I implore you to cleanse my household of all defilement.
If I have spoken it with my mouth,
Or seen it with my eyes,
Or if I have heard it with my ears,
Or stepped on it with my foot,
Or if it has come through my children,
Or my friends, or kinsfolk,
Let it follow these leaves.

88 | *Come and Save Me Because I am Humble*[2]

Thot was the Ibis-God of the ancient Egyptians, one of the numerous
deities in the amalgam of cults that made up ancient Egyptian religion.

---

1. Achebe 1964, p.89.
2. Aafjes 1955, p.80.

He was said to have originated the art of writing and he was worshipped at Hermopolis. This beautiful prayer-poem stresses the need for a worshipful attitude in prayer. Silence and humility bring salvation.

The tall palm tree sixty feet high[1]
Heavy with fruit:
The fruit contains kernels,
The kernels water.
You who bring water to the remotest place,
Come and save me because I am humble.
O Thot, you are a sweet well
For him who starves in the desert,
A well that remains closed to the talkative,
But opens up to the silent.
When the silent man approaches the well reveals itself;
When the noisy man comes you remain hidden.

89 | *Cursing and Forgiving the Prodigal Son*[2]

These are two related texts, in which a Mende father from Sierra Leone first curses his son and asks for his punishment because he has left home without permission, and then welcomes him back after misfortune has brought him to his senses. The son kneels at his father's feet and holds the father's right foot while the curse is removed. Ngewo is the name for the supreme being.

Ah Ngewo, you know this is my son;
I begat him and trained him and laboured for him,
And now that he should do some work for me,
He refuses.
In anything he does now in the world

---

1. The first seven lines of the original are not reproduced in this translation which was made by Ulli Beier, cf. Beier 1966, p.18.
2. Harris 1950, p.283.

May he not prosper
Until he comes back to me
And begs my pardon.

———————

Ah Ngewo, this is my son;
He left me without any good fortune in the world
Because he knows I have cursed him;
He has now come back
To beg me to pull the curse,
As I am pulling now.
Wherever he goes now,
May he prosper and have many children.

90 / *Negative Confession*[1]

This negative, or prudential, confession comes from the Zande of the
Sudan. It is addressed to Mbori, here called 'God'. Mbori is the
'generalized ghost' of the nation as a whole, sharing the rule of the
world with the ancestral ghosts. Water is squirted out of the mouth
before the prayer is said.

Father, as I am here,
I have not stolen the goods of another,
I have not taken the goods of another
Without recompense;
I have not set my heart after the goods of another;
All men are good in my eyes.
God, it is indeed you
Who settles the difference
Between us who are men.

———————

1. Seligman 1932, p.519.

91 / Wherein Have We Erred?[1]

This prayer from the Tumbuka of Malawi was recited during an influenza epidemic. It was a form of confession and offering for sin. The headman and the 'safety doctor' drank from a calabash of fermented gruel and then squirted it from their mouths to right and left, before making the prayer. The prayer is addressed to the ancestors.

> Let the great ones gather!
> What have we done to suffer so?
> We do not say, Let so-and-so come;
> We say, all.
> Here your children are in distress.
> There is not one able to give a drink
>   of water to another.
> Wherein have we erred?
> Here is food; we give to you.
> Aid us, your children!

92 / General Confession[2]

Pastor Robert Sambo of the African National Church composed this general Confession in Tumbuka and Professor Wilson recorded it in translation in Unyakyusa, Tanzania. It assumes a moral unity between traditional religion and Christianity. The prayer replaced the recitation of the Ten Commandments in the Church on occasion.

> Jehovah God, we have come before thee to worship
> And to confess our sins which we have done
>   during the week.

---

1. Young 1950, p.44.
2. Wilson 1959, pp. 194–5

Response
May they all go away.
We have sinned before thee in speaking to people,
We have offended thy creatures
We have spoken bad words,
We have grieved their hearts, Father.

Response
May they all go away.
Our chiefs do not love one another in their hearts.
Take such hearts from them
And give them one heart.

Response
May they all go away.
A new commandment you have given unto us all
To love one another as in heaven
Where there is no quarrelling.
Teach us all to keep thy word, Father.

Response
May they all go away.
That our chiefs may be one in loving
And ruling their country and their people,
And lead us well.
This we pray, Father, grant us.

Response
May they all go away.
The old worship is broken down,
We have come as wild animals
Which are without God.
Call us again to worship, Father.

Response
May they all go away.
Africa is the land of our forefathers.
We have changed her with our new ways,

By leaving all the ways of our forefathers,
Ways which gave peace to the country, Father.
> *Response*
> *May they all go away.*

Our Church is calling everyone to come in
So that the house of marriage may be filled.
It is thy work to give them all new dresses.
> *Response*
> *May they all go away.*

We are taking beer as wild animals;
We forget worship which is our life.
Teach us to drink beer moderately, Father.
> *Response*
> *May they all go away.*

We have forgotten all the laws
You gave to our forefathers.
We have married women by snatching.
Turn us to a life of new marriages
According to the ways of our forefathers, Father.
> *Response*
> *May they all go away.*

Father, Son and Holy Ghost, One God ever and ever.
Amen. Amen. Amen.

93 | *How Has He Erred?*[1]

This Safwa prayer from Tanzania is addressed to the ancestors. 'The
thing which fell up there' is a thunderbolt which struck a house in the
mountains. It is assumed that this event is connected with a past fault.
The worshipper prays for an omen as an answer to his question. How
has his kinsman erred?

---

1. Harwood 1970, p.42.

[Your] Child here claims that the thing
Which fell up there
Broke down the house!
It just missed killing people!
How has he erred?
Indeed, if he has caused things to be disrupted,
Let an omen come.
Tell us that our kinsman has spoiled matters.

94 | Plea for Forgiveness[1]

After a general confession in which individuals admit having committed
certain sins that are called out, the Kono priest of Sierra Leone recites
this prayer before making an offering of cotton, rice and chickens.
After this, the people and their hunting equipment are sprinkled
with water. The Fanu are the ancestral spirits.

O Fanu, if I am for you
And you are for me,
And all the people are for you,
Therefore, you should not be vexed at the people.
Here are the things they have brought
That you may forgive their wrong deeds.

95 | Prayer of the Prisoners[2]

Aubrey Kachingwe offers this sidelight on prison life. Finding himself
in prison, his hero participates in this dialogue act of contrition.
One of the prisoners leads and the others respond. Presumably—

1. Parsons 1964, p.73.
2. Kachingwe 1966, p.175.

though this is not clear from the story—the prayer reflects the traditions of the Cewa of Malawi. It is addressed to the 'God of our forbears' and to 'our ancestors'.

Leader
God of our forbears let us be.
> *Response*
> *We cry before you to lift our troubles.*

Leader
God of the wind, the rain and the earth.
> *Response*
> *We pray, deliver us from our worries.*

Leader
God of hunger, we stole, we fought, we fornicated.
> *Response*
> *We were hungry, so we stole.*
> *We were provoked, so we fought.*
> *She was beautiful, so we sinned.*

Leader
God of mercy, what must we do?
> *Response*
> *We pray, let us free,*
> *And hear the cry of our ancestors . . . .*

96 | *The Shoulders Get Tired of Carrying Sins*[1]

The Zionist Nazarites of South Africa sing hymns such as this one, spontaneously composed to accompany the sacrifice of a 'blessing ox', referred to in the hymn as a 'lamb'. The sacrifice is a thank-offering for a cure from sickness and it is followed by a laying on of hands and a witchcraft cleansing rite, before the communion feast. It is a woman who has been cured.

1. Sundkler 1948, p. 234.

98

Light, thou angel of light,
Thou, mighty one of the road
Which cometh from Jerusalem!
The shoulders get tired of carrying sins,
Oh, help us with this thy lamb,
So that it will be strong and fat,
So that we shall succeed through it,
The day when we bring back thy daughter.

97 | Litany of the Thirteen Questions[1]

This prayer for purity is recited at the annual pilgrimage of the Aladura
Church to Mount Ogere in Monrovia, Liberia. Dr. H. W. Turner
lists three of the thirteen requests. There are subsequent petitions
for mercy, blessing, children, peace, victory, salvation, healing, joy,
God's favour, mighty power of the Spirit and steadfastness. The
Aladura are fond of esoteric names to which they attribute great
power.

Priest
Whence comest ye [sic] hither, ye pilgrims in white robes?
    People
    Tabborrar, Tabborrar, the Mountain of the Lord.
    Tabborrar, Tabborrar, Holy Mountain of Power.
Priest
What is your first request here, ye pilgrims in white robes?
    People
    Forgiveness of our sins from King Ollufijj,
    That God of Tabborrar may forgive all our sins.
Priest
Prayer of forgiveness.
What is your second request here, ye pilgrims in white robes?

---

1.   Turner 1967, p.225.

People
God's cleansing, God's cleansing, Orrewemottola,
That God of Tabborrar may purify us all.
Priest
Prayer.

9. JUDGEMENT

Introduction

It has been asserted that the idea of a 'last judgement' is foreign to African traditional religion, and, while this assertion is probably generally true, it must also be admitted that this idea may have been over-emphasized within the Christian tradition itself. In the Johannine theology, for example, it is clear that the judgement of the world has already begun, and that we are being judged here and now. And even in the theology of Paul and the Synoptics the more eschatalogical view of judgement is balanced by a strong emphasis on an immediate human response to God's offer of salvation. It also seems probable that the different theologies of judgement reflect different human experiences. In times of persecution, when men can find little hope in their present life, they tend to project this hope into the hereafter. There is a difference, therefore, between man in traditional Africa living a present reality or necessity, and the American Negro looking beyond the life and culture which he serves, but of which he cannot be a part.

That being so, one is not surprised to find expressions of hope in the present life among African prayer texts, to find an element of trial or judgement in life itself, and even the idea of a culmination of this trial. We have already noted, in other sections, the picture of the Creator or Supreme Being as judge. In the three texts of this section, all from West Africa, we find the Yoruba of Nigeria teaching the need for mature judgement on the part of man in view of his own culmination in death; we find the Akan of Ghana stressing the aspect of learning from the divine law-giver and finally, the Ewe, also of Ghana, presenting the world as a place of trial with an explicit judgement 'at the gates of the land of death'.

98 | Let Us Not Run The World Hastily[1]

This Yoruba *odu* or recital from Nigeria contains much moral teaching. It advises moderation and mature judgement on the part of men, calmness and due regard for the end of things, even death itself, 'our sleeping'.

> Let us not run the world hastily,
> Let us not grasp at the rope of wealth impatiently;
> What should be treated with mature judgement,
> Let us not treat in a fit of temper;
> Whenever we arrive at a cool place,
> Let us rest sufficiently well;
> Let us give prolonged attention to the future,
> And then let us give due regard to the consequence of things,
> And that is on account of our sleeping.

99 | Good Morning to You, God, I am Learning[2]

This text is a religious drum poem from the Akan of Ghana. It is associated with the awakening ritual that takes place before dawn on a festival day. Learning to abide by God's injunctions can lift the earth and the heavens.

> The heavens are wide, exceedingly wide.
> The earth is wide, very, very wide.
> We have lifted it and taken it away.
> We have lifted it and brought it back.
> From time immemorial,
> The God of old bids us all

1. Idowu 1962, pp.183–4.
2. Nketia 1963, p.44.

Abide by his injunctions.
Then shall we get whatever we want,
Be it white or red.
It is God, the Creator, the Gracious One.
Good morning to you, God, good morning.
I am learning, let me succeed.

100 / *You Will Pass Before a Searching Judge*[1]

This prayer of the Ewe of Ghana is addressed to Mawu, the Creator,
who is the 'Mother of gods' but whose position towards them is
ambivalent. The soul returns after death to Mawu to be judged, and
Mawu sends it back for reincarnation in accordance with the deeds
done in life.

Life is like a hill.
Mawu, the Creator, made it sharp and slippery.
To right and to left deep waters surround it.
You cannot turn back once you start to climb.
You must climb with a load on your head,
A man's arm will not help him, for it is a trial . . . .
At the gates of the land of the dead
You will pass before a searching judge,
His justice is true and he will examine your feet.
He will know how to find every stain
Whether visible or hidden under the skin.
If you have fallen on the way he will know.
If the judge finds no stains on your feet,
Open your belly to joy, for you have overcome
And your belly is clean . . . .
Sickness is the abuse of your well-being;

---

1. Parrinder 1950, pp.233–4.

You will be reminded at the gates of death,
The judge will examine your feet
And you will be punished.

10. PROTECTION FROM EVIL

Introduction

It is, perhaps, not surprising that in a section on protection from
evil the majority of examples should come from religions that emphasize
the cult of guardian spirits and heroes or the protective role of ancestors.
Nevertheless, in only five out of eleven cases is the prayer addressed
to persons other than, or as well as, the Supreme Being, and among the
other examples are three Christian prayers and one Muslim prayer in
which the traditional emphasis on protection is carried forward. All
of this goes to show that protection is a fairly universal value in African
religion, even if it cannot be presented as a single, final explanation
for all prayer.

For the northern Nilotes, the Dinka and Shilluk of Sudan, the
plea for protection is founded on an attitude of trust and intimacy.
For the Dinka, Divinity is the true husband of the home; for the
Shilluk, man is in God's hand. Yet in Shilluk theology, the privileged
position of the hero, Nyikang, already influences the direction of the
petition, for human beings are in Nyikang's hand also. In the other
examples the attitude tends to be negative, even aggressive. Prayer in
these examples is for the exorcism and extirpation of evil, for putting
a stop to the activities of the evil man, and for his punishment.

The Muslim prayer from the Nupe of Nigeria is a straightforward
set of petitions for protection from various eventualities, while the
traditional prayer of the Kenya Nandi expresses the need for constant
prayer to earn the protection of God and the ancestors. In the Christian
Ibo prayer Jesus becomes a protecting spirit, comparable to an ancestor,
while the Zulu prayer uses both Biblical and traditional images of
protection. Finally, the Tiriki Christian hymn from Kenya demonstrates
a fundamental emphasis on protective grace as a bulwark against evil
and sorcery.

This prayer of the Duala of Cameroun is recited at the time of the New Moon. It is a petition for protection from misfortune and from the machinations of wicked men. It ends with a request for prosperity and good social relationships.

> God, be propitious to me!
> Here is the New Moon:
> Keep every harmful sickness far from me.
> Stop the wicked man who is contemplating my mis-
> fortune:
> Let his wicked plans fall on himself.
> O God, be propitious to me!
> Desert me not in my need:
> Give me wives, children, slaves and wealth.
> Lead to my house guests of happiness, O God!

102 / *It Is You Who Protect The Home*[2]

The Dinka of Sudan present Divinity in this prayer as the 'father' and 'husband' of the home. Just as a son propitiates his father after a quarrel, so man must propitiate Divinity, if he is to enjoy his continued protection.

> You protect the homestead,
> Shall I not propitiate you with a cow?
> Divinity, father, you protect the home,
> Husband of the cows,
> Husband of the women,
> It is you who protect the home.

---

1. *Personnalité Africaine et Catholicaisme 1962, p.39.*
2. Lienhardt 1961, p.44.

The Shilluk of Sudan in this prayer praise both God and Nyikang, their hero-ancestor who shares the divine power and to whom the plea for protection is made. Mankind is in God's hands and also in the hands of Nyikang. Sacrifice accompanies the prayer.

> We praise you, you who are God.
>
> Protect us, we are in your hands,
>
> And protect us, save me.
>
> You and Nikawng[2], you are the ones who created.
>
> People are in your hands
>
> And it is you, Nikawng,
>
> Who are accustomed to assist God to save,
>
> And it is you who give the rain.
>
> The sun is yours, and the river is yours,
>
> You who are Nikawng.
>
> You came from under the sun,
>
> You and your father;
>
> You two saved the earth,
>
> And your son Dok[3],
>
> You subdued all the peoples.
>
> The cow is here for you,
>
> And the blood will go to God and you . . . .

104 | *Exorcism Of The Cattle Kraal*[4]

This text accompanies the ritual of the Nyoro of Uganda for building a new cattle kraal. If the omens are favourable, trees are cut for the gateposts and holes for them are dug. After medicine has been thrown into the holes, the posts are rammed home while this prayer is recited.

1. Seligman 1932, p.75.
2. A variant of the more common form Nyikang.
3. A variant of the more common form Dak.
4. Roscoe 1923, p.183.

Bless this tree, make it grow,
Let it be entirely a blessing without any evil.
Remove all evil, let it not come,
But let the good come.
Give thy blessing that we may increase in all things,
And grow wealthy and be free from disease.
Let blessing abound.

105 | *Let Others Be Done By As They Did*[1]

The theme of this Ibo prayer from Nigeria is simple: let others be
done by as they have done to me. The prayer is addressed to God,
but it typically precedes other prayers addressed to the lesser spirits.

God who created man!
My life, the lives of my relatives.
Whoever wishes me to live,
Let him live also.
Whoever wishes me to die,
Let him die.
Whoever wishes that I should have good things,
Let him have them.
Whoever says that I should not eat,
Let his mouth dry up.

106 | *Leave Me Not Behind, Jesus, Wait For Me*[2]

The Nigerian (Ibo) novelist, Chinua Achebe, puts this prayer into the
mouth of Mary in *No Longer At Ease* before the departure of Obi
Okonkwo for studies in England. Jesus is to be the continual companion
and guardian of the one prayed for.

1. Ezeanya 1969, pp.38–9.
2. Achebe 1960, p.11.

Leave me not behind Jesus, wait for me
When I am going to the farm.
Leave me not behind, Jesus, wait for me
When I am going to the market.
Leave me not behind Jesus, wait for me
When I am eating my food.
Leave me not behind Jesus, wait for me
When I am having my bath.
Leave me not behind Jesus, wait for me
When he is going to the White Man's Country.
Leave him not behind Jesus, wait for him.

107 / *Protection In The Rains And Harvest*[1]

These Nupe Muslim prayers from Nigeria were recorded in two
places, Bida and Lemu. The first two stanzas represent prayers at
harvest time, the last two, in the rainy season. Although these are
Muslim prayers, they invoke God by the traditional name Soko,
instead of Allah. They also follow the style of Nupe traditional prayers.

Lord God, protect the house
From the dangers of the harvest season,
Such as falling ill with fever, such as drought.
Give us health. Amin.

The harvest is cleared:
Soko protect us from fire;
Soko protect us from small-pox;
Soko protect us from the heat that dries up everything.

Soko, may he give rain in plenty.
May he give food that thrives beautifully.
The grain, may it thrive beautifully.
Soko, send water which falls down upon man.

1. Nadel 1954, pp.238–9.

And the man who is in a canoe on the water,
And the water in the bush,
Protect them also for all of us.

Lord God, protect us from the danger
Which is in the rain and the storms,
And also the lightning.
Protect the house from it.
Give us health. Amin.

108 | *Hearken To My Constant Prayer*[1]

This is a free, metric translation of a common prayer from the Nandi
of Kenya. It is used especially by old men on rising, particularly after a
bad dream during the night. The prayer sees divine protection as the
reward of constant prayer.

O God, do thou thine ear incline,
Protect my children and my kine,
E'en if thou'rt weary, still forbear,
And hearken to my constant prayer.
When shrouded 'neath the cloak of night,
Thy splendours sleep beyond our sight,
And when across the sky by day,
Thou movest, still to thee I pray.
Dread shades of our departed sires,
Ye who can make or mar desires,
Slain by no mortal hand ye dwell,
Beneath the earth, O guard us well.

---

1. Hollis 1909, p.42.

Among the Kono of Sierra Leone, the Bengene, or purification priest, occupies an important position. For the purification of the forest, prayer is offered through deceased priests to other heavenly beings that they have addressed in their lifetime. A fowl is immolated and its blood dropped on to stone images, after which medicine is sprinkled towards the forest. The chief effect desired is protection from evil.

> O Meketa, Seven Heavens, Seven Earths,
> Fakumu, Faiyande, Heavenly Children:
> Whether or not I know how to make this sacrifice,
> You will trouble the one who does not know how,
> But the person who knows how, will have no trouble.
> Therefore, I ask you to hold all evil from us.
> Make it blind; make it lame;
> Carry it to the spirit in the mountain.
> Put it in a deep pit; place a stone upon it;
> Let the good wind from the north and the south
> And from the rising to the setting sun blow upon it.
> Let it be so, for you are able to do this.
> The heavenly children are offering this sacrifice.
> They are calling.
> Whether or not I know how to make this sacrifice,
> You know when I am free.
> You are my helper, my lifter.

110 / Hatch Us, Wondrous Hen[2]

The eagle is a traditional symbol of powerful protection among the Zulu of South Africa. In this hymn of the Zionist Nazarites this symbol

1. Parsons 1964, p.74.
2. Sundkler 1948, pp.293-4.

is mixed with the humbler, Gospel symbol of the mother-hen gathering
her chicks under her wing.

O mountain eagle,
Lift thy mighty wing;
We need thy shelter,
Thou rock of our father.

We have no fortress
Other than thee
In which to find shelter,
We thy wayward creatures.

We stand before thee,
O beautiful hen.
Thou dost not love
Jerusalem now.

O love us and hatch us
Wondrous hen!
We dwell in thy kingdom,
Our hen of heaven.

O Lord bring it forth
This Ekuphakameni,[1]
Just as a hen
Loveth her chickens.

O Jerusalem, Jerusalem,
How great was my longing
To gather thy children
Under my wing,
But they would not.
Thus art thou left desolate.

---

1. Headquarters of the Church.

The Tiriki in Kenya feel that constant prayer affords a protection against evil and sorcery. This spontaneous, dancing hymn came originally from the Dini ya Roho (Religion of the Spirit) and was adopted by the African Israel Church in the 1950s. It prays for grace for different groups of Christians. The names can be varied at will.

> The Israels today need grace.
>
> The Israels today need grace.
>
> The Salvation Army members today need grace.
>
> The Friends today need grace.
>
> The Pentecostals today need grace . . . .

11. CELESTIAL SYMBOLS OF PROSPERITY AND GOOD FORTUNE

Introduction

It is well known that sky symbolism is associated with theistic belief, and many African peoples employ a celestial symbol for the Supreme Being or Creator, be it the sun, the lightning, the rainbow or the sky itself. The first text in this section offers an example of this in the Karimojong of Uganda who call their Deity *akuj*, sky. Sunshine and sky symbolism generally are rather obvious symbols of good fortune, especially among people who depend so heavily on the elements of nature, and the idea of the Supreme Being as the source of benevolence and luck is certainly present in the symbolism.

The prayer texts, however, seem to reflect a stronger emphasis on celestial phenomena as symbols of prosperity and good fortune among peoples whose notion of the Supreme Being is more complex, or who have a multiplicity of powers standing in a somewhat ambivalent relationship to the Creator. For the Luyia of Kenya, the sun is a

---

1. Sangree 1966, p.210.

symbol of blessing, while for the Bushmen of South Africa, the moon is a symbol of success in hunting and of happiness on either side of the grave. For the Yoruba of Nigeria, beauty in general is best exemplified by all the astral bodies which are in turn symbols of riches and good fortune. Like the Bushmen, the Ngombe of Zaire pray to the moon for luck. In their case, the occasion is a fishing expedition or the ambition to make money. It is interesting to see this association carried over from African tradition into two Christian texts from Ghana.

112 | *The Cloud-Spotted Sky Has Heard*[1]

The following litany was recorded among the pastoralist Karimojong of Uganda at an initiation sacrifice. The prayer-leader walks round the enclosure leading the litany and calling for good fortune. Different leaders succeed each other, and the petitions are repeated. God is symbolized by the cloud-spotted sky. The initiates are called 'Gazelles'.

> The Gazelles: I say the Gazelles. There are Gazelles.
> These people, the Gazelles which are here, they have become big!
> *Response*
> *They have become big!*
> The mountains also. There are mountains.
> *Response*
> *There are!*
> There are!
> *Response*
> *There are!*
> The Karimojong also, they are.
> *Response*
> *They are!*
> There are Karimojong.

---

1. Dyson-Hudson 1966, pp.165–7.

Response
There are!

Cattle as well. The cattle of the mountains. They are.

Response
They are!

The cattle, the cattle of the mountains, they become fat.

Response
They are fat!

They become fat. Do they not become fat?

Response
They are fat!

The land. This land here. Does it not become good?

Response
It is good!

In this country there are Gazelles.

Response
There are!

The mountains also they are.

Response
They are!

Ngipian [clan] also. They are here, are they not?

Response
They are!

In this land here, they are.

Response
They are!

There is well-being in our country, is there not?

Response
There is!

It is here.

Response
It is!

Yes. Evil is going away.

Response
It has gone !
Well-being is with us.
Response
It is !
It will always be with us, will it not?
Response
It will !
It will.
Response
It will !
Will it not?
Response
It will !
God [Sky] has heard.
Response
He has heard !
He has heard.
Response
He has heard !
The Sky, the cloud-spotted sky here, it has heard.
Response
It has heard !

113 | *Bring Riches Today As The Sun Rises*[1]

The Luyia of Kenya address both God and the Sun in this prayer, and
it is clear that, while it is part of creation, the Sun is a symbol of God's
blessing. This is a purification prayer recited at sunrise. It asks for
guidance in work, for health, riches and good fortune.

O Sun,
As you rise in the east through God's leadership,

1. Yokoo 1966, p.66.

Wash away all the evils I have thought of throughout the night.
Bless me, so that my enemies will not kill me and my family;
Guide me through hard work.
O God, give me mercy upon our children who are suffering,
Bring riches today as the sun rises;
Bring all fortunes to me today.

114 | Prayer to the Moon for Luck[1]

The Bushman hunter-gatherers pray to the heavenly bodies, especially the moon, which is said to have been created by the Sky God out of his shoe. The waxing and waning of the moon gives assurance of life and rebirth after death. Life depends on finding food and so the moon is approached to help man find food, in this case an ostrich egg.

Ho, Moon lying there,
Let me early tomorrow see an ostrich;
As the ostrich sits on the eggs.
Let me whisk out the yolk
With a gemsbok tail hair,
Which sits together upon a little stick,
Upon which the gemsbok tail sits.

115 | Prayer to the Moon for Success in Hunting[2]

Like the previous prayer this is also addressed by Bushmen people to the moon. It is the simple prayer of the huntsman for success in finding food. Game is an important element in the diet of the South African Bushmen and life depends on successful hunting.

---

1. Bleek 1929, p.306.
2. Bleek 1929, p.306.

Ho, Moon lying there,
Let me kill a springbok,
Tomorrow
Let me eat spingbok;
With this arrow
Let me shoot a springbok!

116 | *Prayer to the Moon for Immortality*[1]

This is an even more poignant prayer to the moon than the preceding two from South Africa. It is an explicit prayer for life after death after the pattern of the waxing and waning moon, a Bushman symbol of immortality.

Take my face and give me yours!
Take my face, my unhappy face.
Give me your face,
With which you return
When you have died,
When you vanished from sight.
You lie down and return—
Let me resemble you, because you have joy,
You return ever more alive,
After you vanished from sight.
Did you not promise me once
That we too should return
And be happy again after death?

117 | *Prayer to the Young Moon*[2]

Once again the Bushman hunter-gatherer addresses the moon in this prayer, asking for success in the hunt, for 'a little thing that I may eat'.

1. Schmidt 1933, p.557.
2. Bleek and Lloyd 1911, p.181.

Young Moon!
Hail, Young Moon!
Hail, hail,
Young Moon!
Young Moon! Speak to me!
Tell me of something,
Hail, hail.
When the sun rises
Thou must speak to me
That I may eat something.
Thou must speak to me about a little thing,
That I may eat.
Hail, hail,
Young Moon!

118 | Who Does Not Look On Beauty Soon Is Poor[1]

This is a religious poem of the Yoruba of Nigeria praising the divination figure Iwori Wotura, symbol of good fortune and beauty, ideas which are linked in Yoruba thought. This figure is the praise of all Ifa divination, and of Olódùmaré, the Supreme Being. It is likened to the beauties of creation including the rainbow, the moon and the stars.

Iwori Wotura,
Anybody who meets beauty and does not look at it
Will soon be poor.
The red feathers are the pride of the parrot.
The young leaves are the pride of the palm tree,
Iwori Wotura.
The straight tree is the pride of the forest.
The fast deer is the pride of the bush,

---

1. Beier 1970, p.48.

Iwori Wotura.

The rainbow is the pride of heaven.

The beautiful woman is the pride of her husband,

Iwori Wotura.

The children are the pride of the mother.

The moon and the stars are the pride of the sun,

Iwori Wotura.

Ifa says: Beauty and all sorts of good fortune arrive.

119 | Prayer for Good Fortune[1]

This prayer of the Ga of Ghana is recited at the annual corn-planting feast. It follows a goat sacrifice and is addressed to Nyongmo, the Supreme Being, whose symbol is rain, and to Mamu, God of the Sea. The prayer is for good fortune and the blessing of water receives special mention.

Hail, hail, hail. Let happiness come.

Our stools and our brooms . . .

If we dig a well, may it be at a spot where water is.

If we take water to wash our shoulders may we be refreshed.

Nyongmo, give us blessing.

Mamu, give us blessing.

May the town be blest.

May the Agbafo [religious officials] be blessed.

May the Wulomei [high priests] be blest.

May the Woyei [priests] be blest.

May we be filled, going and coming.

May we not drop our head-pads except at the big pot.

May our fruitful women be like gourds

And may they bring forth and sit down.

---

1. Field 1937, p.30.

May misfortunes jump over us.

If today anyone takes up a stick or a stone against this our
   blessing,

Do we bless him?

May Sunday and Wednesday kill him,

May we flog him.

Hail, let happiness come.

Is our voice one?

Hail, let happiness come.

120 | God Has Given Me Good Luck[1]

For the Ambo of South West Africa, Kalunga (God) is an unapproach-
able, but infinitely powerful, great chief. This prayer expresses relief
at the recovery of a sick man from illness, seen as the victory of God
over an evil spirit.

God has given me good luck,
My man has got better;
God is stronger than the spirit,
He chased him out.

121 | Prayer To The New Moon[2]

For the Ngombe of Zaïre the moon is a special object of veneration
as a symbol of good fortune in a religious system which places an
equal emphasis on a direct approach to the Supreme Being, and on an
indirect approach through ancestral and other spirits. This prayer takes
the form of a greeting to the new moon.

---

1.   Smith 1950, p.146.
2.   Smith 1950, p.177

The New Moon shines;
I show thee my right hand;
I show thee my left hand;
If I go fishing with thee may I kill many;
If I look for money with thee
May I get much money.

122 / Open The Windows Of Heaven[1]

This hymn comes from the Fante Methodist Church in Ghana.
It is a lyric or apostrophe that interrupts a sermon, and the idea it
conveys of a shower of blessings from the sky is very much in the spirit
of traditional African prayers. It is addressed to Onyame [God].

Open the windows of heaven,
Give us thy blessing!
Open the windows of heaven,
Give us thy blessing!
Our Father, Onyame,
Sweet Father of us, the Church membership.
Open the windows of heaven,
Give us thy blessing!

123 / Prayer For The Good Fortune Of Work[2]

This Christian prayer from Takoradi on the Ghana coast was composed
by a harbour man out of work. The sunshine and the steamers are
there, but there is not enough work for everyone.

The day is there and the sunshine,
With steamers in the harbour,

---

1. Williamson 1958, p.129.
2. Pawelzik 1968, p.42.

But is there work?
Others have friends,
Others have money.
They can drain their whisky bottle,
And I stand nearby unemployed.
Dear God, can't you give me work in the harbour?
To have money for wife and children.
To put my little bit in your basket next Sunday.
Please give me work, good Lord Jesus.
We praise you. Amen.

12. PEACE, INTERNAL AND EXTERNAL

Introduction

The texts in this section reveal a sophisticated idea of peace—not the idea of 'peace and plenty' alone, but a peace which is the outcome of self-control, good order and social harmony. The fact that the majority of the texts come from peoples whose religious beliefs and practices are markedly theistic does not mean that other peoples do not value inner peace. On the contrary, there is plenty of evidence that the banishing of feelings of enmity and suppressed anger are a necessary pre-condition for worship among a large number of peoples. However, the theistic religions do appear to emphasize inner states and moral relationships, perhaps more than the others.

For the Boran of Kenya and the Galla of Ethiopia peace is the antithesis of pride and calumny, of theft and murder, but it is also the outcome of a state of continual prayer to God, the only author of peace and prosperity. For the Kikuyu of Kenya peace includes unity and social order, and is typically a state of calmness and freedom from unpleasant surprises. For the Nuer of the Sudan social tranquillity depends on the 'coolness of soul', and the Ga of Ghana re-echo the Kikuyu petition for a unity of voices. Finally, from Ghana come two applications of this traditional call for unity to contemporary situations. A Christian prayer asks for unity among Christians and within the Christian churches themselves, and another prayer calls for harmony in commercial relationships based on justice.

124 / *Let Me Pass The Day In Peace*[1]

This beautiful morning prayer of the Boran of Kenya, asks not so much for a prosperous peace, as for one which flows from a good conscience and from a continuous attitude of prayer.

> O God, thou hast let me pass the night in peace,
> Let me pass the day in peace.
> Wherever I may go
> Upon my way which thou madest peaceable for me,
> O God, lead my steps.
> When I have spoken,
> Keep off calumny from me.
> When I am hungry,
> Keep me from murmuring.
> When I am satisfied,
> Keep me from pride.
> Calling upon thee, I pass the day,
> O Lord who hast no Lord.

125 / *Let Me Pass The Night In Peace*[2]

An evening prayer of the Boran of Kenya which corresponds to the last (morning) prayer. It takes up and develops the final invocation of that prayer, 'O Lord who hast no Lord'.

> O God, thou hast let me pass the day in peace,
> Let me pass the night in peace,
> O Lord who hast no Lord.

---

1. Tutschek 1845, pp.87–8.
2. Tutschek 1845, p.88.

There is no strength but in thee.
Thou alone hast no obligation.
Under thy hand I pass the night.
Thou art my mother and my father.

126 | O God, Lead My Steps[1]

Like the two previous texts, this lengthy prayer of the Boran of Kenya
asks for peace under the direction of an inscrutable God who permits
infringements of peace at the hands of violent men, but who demands
ultimate trust in his providence.

Good God of this earth, my Lord!
Thou art above me, I am below thee.
When misfortune comes to me,
As trees keep off the sun from me,
Mayest thou keep off misfortune;
My Lord, be thou my shadow!
Calling upon thee, I pass the day.
Calling upon thee, I pass the night.
When this moon rises, do not forsake me;
When I rise, I do not forsake thee;
Let the danger pass by me.
God, my Lord, thou Sun with thirty rays,
When the enemy comes,
Let not thy worm be killed upon the earth;
Keep him off, as we seeing a worm upon the earth,
Crush him if we like, spare him if we like.
As we tread upon and kill a worm upon the earth,
Thus, if thou pleasest, thou crushest us upon the earth.

---

1. Tutschek 1845, pp.84–7.

God, thou goest, holding the bad and the good in thy hand;
My Lord, let us not be killed,
We thy worms, we are praying to thee.
A man who knows not evil and good may not anger thee;
If once he knew it and was not willing to know it,
This is wicked—treat him as it pleases thee.
If he formerly did not learn,
Do thou, my Lord, teach him.
If he learns not the language of men,
He learns thy language.
God, thou hast made all the animals and men
That live upon the earth;
The corn also upon this earth on which we are to live
Hast thou made; we have not made it.
Thou hast given us strength;
Thou hast given us cattle and corn;
We worked with them and the seed grew up for us.
With the corn which thou let'st grow for us
Men were satisfied.
The corn in the house has been burnt up;
Who has burnt the corn in the house?
Thou knowest.
If I know one or two men,
I know them when I have seen them with my eye;
Thou, even if thou didst not see them with thine eyes,
Knowest them by thy heart.
A single bad man has chased away all our people from their
    houses;
The children and their mother has he scattered
Like a flock of turkeys, hither and thither.
The murderous enemy took the curly-headed child
Out of his mother's hand and killed him.
Thou hast permitted all this to be done so.

Why hast thou done so?
Thou knowest.
The corn which thou let'st grow
Dost thou show to our eyes;
The hungry man looks at it and is comforted.
When the corn blooms thou sendest butterflies
And locusts into it—locusts and doves.
All this comes from thy hand;
Thou hast caused it to be done so.
Why hast thou done so?
Thou knowest.
My Lord, spare those who pray to thee!
As a thief, stealing another's corn,
Is bound by the owner of the corn,
Thus do not thou bind, O Lord;
Binding the beloved one thou settest free with love.
If I am beloved by thee,
So set me free, I entreat thee from my heart;
If I do not pray to thee with my heart,
Thou hearest me not.
If I pray to thee with my heart,
Thou knowest it and art gracious unto me.

127 | *Litany for Peace*[1]

This litany for peace, with its recurring response, is typical of the kind of prayer recited by the Kikuyu of Kenya at a public assembly. Except in the case of urgent need, it was not accompanied by sacrifice. The first petition is for wisdom and the ability to speak with one voice. The Supreme Being is addressed as Ngai.

> Say ye, the elders may have wisdom and speak with one
> voice.

1. Kenyatta 1938, p.238.

Praise ye, Ngai. Peace be with us.

Say ye that the country may have tranquillity

And the people may continue to increase.

Praise ye, Ngai. Peace be with us.

Say ye that the people and the flocks and the herds

May prosper and be free from illness.

Praise ye, Ngai. Peace be with us.

Say ye the fields may bear much fruit

And the land may continue to be fertile.

Praise ye, Ngai. Peace be with us.

128 | Prayer Against Unpleasant Surprises[1]

This harvesting prayer of the Kikuyu of Kenya was recited by elders
facing the sacred mountain, Mount Kenya. It followed the sacrifice
of a lamb under a ritual fig-tree. The prayer is addressed to God,
Mwene Nyaga (possessor of brightness) and asks for peace and an
assurance against unpleasant surprises.

Mwene Nyaga, you who have brought us rain

And has given us good harvest,

Let people eat grain of this harvest calmly and peacefully.

Do not bring us any surprise or depression.

Guard us against illness of people or our herds and flocks;

So that we may enjoy this season's harvest in tranquillity.

Peace, praise ye Ngai, peace be with us.

129 | Let the Souls of Thy People be Cool[2]

This text is typical of the short, petitionary prayers used by the Nuer
of Sudan to introduce the longer invocations at a sacrifice. It is also a

1. Kenyatta 1938, p.258.
2. Evans-Pritchard, 1956, p.22.

form used in spontaneous, private prayer. This particular prayer is a stock petition for peace of heart and freedom from evil, addressed to Spirit or Kwoth.

> Our Father, it is thy Universe,
> It is thy will, let us be at peace,
> Let the souls of thy people be cool;
> Thou art our Father,
> Remove all evil from our path.

130 | Are Our Voices One ?[1]

This hymn of the Ga of Ghana accompanies the Kple tradition of worship, defined by a certain type of dancing. It follows a libation of rum. Akpitioko is the goddess of Kple dancing, and Awudu is an animal god—the horned, black, spitting snake—said to be the son of Sakumo. The Father Rain-God is Ata Nyongmo, the Supreme Being, while Otshiama has vanished from memory and tradition. Peace and happiness depend here on unity.

> Hail, hail, hail, let happiness come!
> Are our voices one ?
> Let Grandfather Sakumo give peace.
> Let Akpitioko give peace.
> Let Otshiama give peace.
> Let Awudu the Almighty give peace.
> Let Father Rain-God give peace.
> Hail, hail, hail, let happiness come!

131 | Prayer for Christian Unity[2]

This prayer composed by a Ghanaian Christian asks for unity within

---

1. Field 1937, p.14.
2. Pawelzik 1968, p.75.

and between the churches. The author sees unity as essentially an African characteristic, and division as having been imported from Europe.

> Lord, your churches quarrel,
> Bishops feel superior,
> Behave as if they were Our Lord himself,
> From Europe they import traditions
> And book-learning.
> We don't want their division.
> We want one Church.
> Lord, has your Son not prayed for this one Church?
> Lord, we ask you for one Church in Ghana,
> One Church in Africa.
> We are on our way.
> Give us so much love in our heart
> That the separation will be drowned in it.
> Amen.

132 | Peace Between Buyer and Seller[1]

Another Christian prayer from Ghana. This time the importance of harmony between buyers and sellers is stressed. On the one hand, a readiness to pay the value of the goods, on the other, a refusal to over-charge and cause poor people to go hungry, are prayed for.

> Buyers and sellers,
> Lord, you know, in our country,
> These people are quite special,
> But nobody can fool you,
> Neither the buyer nor those who sell.

---

1. Pawelzik 1968, p.45.

It is not just a trifle
Over which we can make merry.
There can be fraud whilst people are hungry.
Others pile up their riches.
Lord, whether we buy or sell,
Let us stick to this.
We are quite willing to pay
The value of the goods,
But others should not overcharge.
Lord, make peace here as well.
Amen.

13. VICTORY AND WAR

Introduction

Remarkably few prayers which deal with the subject of war have been recorded by ethnographers. Probably, this was because the era of tribal wars was over by the time that fieldwork began. Nevertheless the few specimens that can be found justify treatment on their own. The Kikuyu example from Kenya smacks of over-confidence and complacency, but sentiments of gratitude, of zeal and loyalty, compete in the text with the petition for victory against the enemy. The prayer of the Nuer from Sudan is less truculent, but nonetheless vindictive in its hatred for the Nuba peoples and the British colonial masters.

Finally, the Mende texts illustrate an interesting, traditional account of the origin of prayer itself, which turns out in the end to be a petition for life and the preservation of life, particularly in time of war.

133 | Help Us Keep Our Enemies At Bay[1]

Jomo Kenyatta puts this long prayer into the mouths of the Kikuyu warriors of Kenya. It was the kind of prayer recited in the war camp—

1. Kenyatta 1966, pp.23-4.

a mixture of thanks, a petition for victory and a pledge of zeal and loyalty.

> O our heavenly Great Elder, we are thankful for the natural gifts which you have bestowed upon us, unlike the lands of our neighbours, some of which you passed over in a hurry, and threw one river here and another there, leaving the rest of the country dry and in many places unforested. Remembering this, we surely believe that, even as you gave us all the good things of life, you will, no doubt, always give us wisdom to make good strong spears, and to sharpen them as well. O Mwene Nyaga, you will give us strength so that when our enemies come to close quarters we will be able, with your guidance and our strong muscles, to drive our spears right through their hearts, and prevent them from depriving us of the gifts which you, the Lord of Nature, have bestowed upon us. We pledge to you, O Mwene Nyaga, that we shall not sit idle and let anyone snatch away what you have promised to our forefathers, to be our children's birthright for ever.

134 | Battle Hymn[1]

Among the Nuer of Sudan the spirits of the air, Deng, Dayim and Mani, are associated with war. This hymn prays that the members of the Jagei tribe may defeat the people of the Nuba hills two years in succession and strike down the British. It is recited in honour of a person struck by lightning and probably dates from the beginning of British occupation. It exults in victory over the Dinka but takes the humble title of 'ants' before the spirits.

> Stars and moon which are in the heavens,
> Blood of Deng which you have taken,
> You have not summoned the ants of Deng capriciously,

---

1. Evans-Pritchard 1956, pp.46–7.

Blood of Deng which you have taken.
The wing of battle on the river bank is encircled by plumes.
Dayim, son of God, strike the British to the ground.
Break the steamer on the Nile and let the British drown.
Kill the people on the mountains [Nuba Hills],
Kill them twice.
Do not slay them jestingly.
Mani goes with a rush,
He goes on forever.
The sons of Jagei are proud in the byres,
Proud that they always raid the Dinka.

135 | Let Not Our Town Be Spoiled By War[1]

These texts illustrate the tradition of how the Mende of Sierra Leone first started to pray. Ngewo (God) made a big mountain (his oracle) to speak to human beings. It appeared in the form of an old man and demanded food. The visionary promises service, performs the service he promised, and then begs for life and for an end to war.

> Big mountain, big mountain,
> I have come to you here.
> I have come to tell you,
> The big pot you asked for,
> We are coming with it tomorrow.
> Therefore, however high the sun may go up tomorrow,
> Do not go anywhere until I come.
> If it looks quiet, I have not yet come.

———

> Big mountain, big mountain,
> The big pot I spoke of yesterday,

---

1. Harris 1950, p.289.

I have brought it.
I said, do not go away until we came,
No matter how high the sun was.
Now we have come.
The rice we have brought is not enough for everybody.
Who must eat it, the men or the women?

———————

O Big mountain, we did not put you to shame.
We all came here today.
If there is anyone sick amongst us, make him well;
And our children, let not the witch people,
Or any other evil attack them.
Let no one bring war to us.
Let not our town be spoiled by war;
Let none of us be lost in war.
Let our women not die at childbirth.

14. CRISIS AND DESPERATION

Introduction

Differences of emphasis in the various religious systems of traditional
Africa do not much affect prayers made at moments of crisis and
desperation. This is because, even in those religions in which the
Supreme Being normally appears not to play any direct role in people's
lives, he is approached in moments of crisis. The texts in this section
illustrate the various kinds of crisis that can occur and which are the
occasion for this kind of prayer.

The first example from the Meru of Kenya is part of this people's
historical tradition of a critical moment in their journey to their present
territory on the Kenya mainland. The second text, from the Kikuyu
of Kenya, is a prayer of despair from one who prays for death. The
Dinka prayers arise out of occasions of social disharmony and serious
illness; while the final prayer from the Nyamwezi of Tanzania is the

cry of a rain-maker whose whole reputation is threatened because of
drought. This is an interesting variation on the theme of most of the
other prayers which are concerned with famine, hunger and drought,
scourges that are all too frequent in tropical Africa. The only exception
is the prayer from Burundi which illustrates another desperate condition
that is particularly feared in Africa, that of barrenness.

136 | *Prayer of the Meru Exodus*[1]

According to the tradition of the Meru of Kenya, they crossed from
an off-shore island on to the Kenya mainland at the dawn of their
history. This prayer was made by the Mugwe, their prophet-leader,
at the moment of fording the channel.

> One body and possessor of strength,
> Give me thy help,
> That I may lead this people of thine
> Free from all their sufferings.

137 | *Prayer for the Release of Death*[2]

Mukami, in James Ngugi's story 'The Fig Tree', wanders alone in the
forests of Kikuyu, Kenya. She asks Murungu, the God of the Kikuyu
ancestors, Gikuyu and Mumbi, who dwells on Kerinyaga, to come with
the spirits of the dead, and take her. She asks Earth also to swallow
her like the Gumba pygmies who lived in underground tunnels and
under tree roots.

> Oh Spirits of the dead, come for me!
> Oh Murungu, God of Gikuyu and Mumbi,

---

1. Bernardi 1959, p.202.
2. Ngugi 1965, p.74.

Who dwells on high Kerinyaga, yet is everywhere,
Why don't you release me from misery?
Dear Mother Earth, why don't you open and swallow me up?
Even as you had swallowed Gumba—
The Gumba who disappeared under Mikongoe roots?

138 / Divinity, Help Me[1]

This is part of a hymn from the Dinka of Sudan. It is the complaint of an anxious child to his father, Divinity. In spite of the protection of the clan-divinity Deng-Yath, everything in the family is going wrong because of lies and confusion.

> I have been left in misery indeed.
> Divinity, help me!
> Will you refuse the ants of this country?
> When we have the clan-divinity Deng,
> Our home is called 'Lies and Confusion'.
> What is all this for, O Divinity?
> Alas, I am your child.

139 / Prayer of the Sick Man[2]

For the Dinka of Sudan, the free divinity, Deng, possesses many modes of existence. 'Great Deng' or Dengdit, is a way of referring to Divinity himself. This prayer asks that the sick man be not abandoned to the power of sickness.

> Deng of my father,
> Deng of surpassing greatness.
> My father Deng,

---

1. Lienhardt 1961, p.45.
2. Lienhardt 1961, p.94.

A great person through the ages.

Great Deng refuses.

Great Deng refuses.

If not honoured, he is offended, indifferent.

My father Deng, do not forsake me,

My father Deng, do not abandon me to the power.

140 | *Desperate Plea For Offspring*[1]

This cry for help is known as *kwambaza* in Burundi, and it comes from
a person in great distress, in this case, barrenness. Imana is the Supreme
Being for the Hutu and Tutsi ethnic groups. People in distress go
to the stream and lie in wait for Imana to come in the form of a calf.

O Imana of Urundi,

If only you would help me!

O Imana of pity,

Imana of my father's house,

If only you would help me!

O Imana of the country of the Hutu and Tutsi,

If only you would help me just this once!

O Imana, if only you would give me

A homestead and children!

I prostrate myself before you,

Imana of Urundi.

I cry to you: Give me offspring,

Give me as you give to others!

Imana, what shall I do, where shall I go?

I am in distress,

Where is there room for me?

O merciful, O Imana of mercy,

Help this once.

---

1. Guillebaud 1950, pp.192–3.

Gauwa, the God of the Bushmen of South Africa, is thought to appear in thunder and lightning. This prayer comes from a frustrated hunter who still hopes that God will provide an animal.

> Gauwa must help us that we kill an animal.
> Gauwa, help us.
> We are dying of hunger.
> Gauwa does not give us help.
> He is cheating.
> He is bluffing.
> Gauwa will bring something for us to kill next day,
> After he himself hunts and has eaten meat,
> When he is full and is feeling well.

142 / *Prayer for Rain*[2]

Tsui-Goab is the hero-ancestor of the Hottentots of South Africa, and he is said to have fought against the Spirit of the Dead, Gaunab. Tsui-Goab replaces the concept of a Supreme Provider in this prayer against Drought.

> Thou, O Tsui-Goab!
> Father of our fathers,
> Thou, our father!
> Let the thunder-cloud stream!
> Let our flocks live!
> Let us also live please!

---

1. Marshall 1962, p.247.
2. Schmidt 1933, p.628.

I am so very weak indeed
From thirst,
From hunger!
Let me eat field fruits!
Art thou not our father?
The father of the fathers,
Thou, Tsui-Goab.
That we may praise thee!
That we may bless thee!
Thou father of the fathers!
Thou, our Lord!
Thou, oh, Tsui-Goab!

143 | I Lie Down Without Food[1]

Another prayer of a desperate huntsman, who prepares to lie down after
an unsuccessful and hungry day. This text comes from one of the
Tswana tribes in Lesotho. The worshipper will be content with even
the smallest answer to his prayer.

God of my fathers,
I lie down without food,
I lie down hungry,
Although others have eaten
And lie down full.
Even if it be but a polecat,
Or a little rock-rabbit,
I shall be grateful.
I cry to God, father of my ancestors.

---

1.   Smith 1950, p.121.

The Nyamwezi rain-maker in Tanzania is the repository of God's power over rain. In this case, the rain-maker feels his power is failing. He prays not to the source of his power, but to the ancestor from whom he inherited it. The prayer accompanies rain rites which involve the pouring of water, and the sacrifice of a goat and sheep.

> O Chief who have left me in this world at your death,
> I come to offer the sacrifices.
> Rain has ceased to fall in our country long ago.
> Give us rain! Here is your water!
> Give us rain! Let it rain!
> Why do you leave me in trouble, you my Lord?
> I have inherited your power. I did not usurp it.
> You have left me in trouble.
> If you [continue] and it does not rain in the land,
> The inhabitants will go away.
> Look, here is the goat, and here is your sheep!

15. OLD AGE AND DEATH

Introduction

The majority of these prayers about old age and death come from peoples among whom the ancestor cult is pronounced. For settled peoples with territorial possessions and with the graves of their forbears among them, death is a more constant reality, and possibly, more of a problem. In African myths about the origin of death, death is not so explicitly associated with human sin, as is the case in Christianity. People in Africa have not, traditionally, been ready to accept death as a punishment for their own and others' shortcomings. On the other hand, the kind of death suffered—particularly an early death—is thought to be related to the dead man's actions. In this sense, as the

1. Dammann 1962, p.118.

third Yoruba text shows, death is an implicit judgement on life in the world. If one behaves gently, one will die peacefully and receive a decent burial as well as offerings from one's children. Death is known to be a transition to another state of life, but this second state depends on how well the opportunities one has received in this life are used. Man prays, therefore, for a long life in which to have many children and build up possessions. As the Ambo of South West Africa put it, the grave must be well prepared. On the other hand, there is also the element of shock and hopelessness among the living when confronted by the death of someone close to them. 'The gates of the underworld are closed.' It is now in dreams and visions that one will meet one's dear ones who have departed. Nevertheless, the hope exists of meeting in the next life, and of having a place prepared there. The independent churches tend to have a negative attitude to death. In the example from the Aladura Church of West Africa the Biblical emphasis on preparedness is combined with the traditional plea for more time.

145 | *The Gates of the Underworld are Closed*[1]

This Bushman religious poem from South Africa reflects an attitude of hopeless despair in front of death. The dead wait passively for God to say 'Come' or 'Go'.

> The gates of the underworld are closed.
> Closed are the gates.
> The spirits of the dead are thronging together
> Like swarming mosquitoes in the evening,
> Like swarming mosquitoes.
> Like swarms of mosquitoes dancing in the evening,
> When the night has turned black, entirely black,
> When the sun has sunk, has sunk below,
> When the night has turned black,
> The mosquitoes are swarming

---

1. Trilles 1932, pp.429–30.

Like whirling leaves,
Dead leaves in the wind.
Dead leaves in the wind,
They wait for him who will come,
For him who will come and will say:
'Come' to the one and 'Go' to the other;
And God will be with his children.
And God will be with his children.

146 | Prayer For A Happy Old Age[1]

In this prayer, the Yoruba of Nigeria ask for a happy old age, not a
wretched twilight of life in which they have to scavenge for food in the
place of sacrifices, an omen of the fewness of offerings after death.

That we may not die young;
That we may not attain an old age of wretchedness;
That we may not scratch the ground with a stick
In the place of sacrifices.

147 | A Long Farewell[2]

This short religious poem from the Yoruba of Nigeria celebrates the
change in human relationships wrought by death. It is now in visions
on lonely roads and in dreams that the living will encounter their
loved ones.

It is a long farewell!
It is now a matter of meeting along the road,
It is now in dreams.

1. Idowu 1962, p.185.
2. Idowu 1962, p.185.

148 / *Prayer For A Happy Death*[1]

Another short religious poem from the Yoruba of Nigeria, exhorting men to behave gently in this life so that they may have a peaceful death and a loving funeral from their relatives, and invocations after death.

> Let us behave gently,
> That we may die peacefully;
> That our children may stretch out their hands
> Upon us in burial.

149 / *We Are Bereft of a Leader*[2]

This funeral dirge from the Akan of Ghana expresses hopelessness in the face of death. The people are bereft of their leader. Parents and everyone are being carried away by death. This dirge is sung on the lorry that is carrying the corpse to the funeral.

> We are bereft of a leader,
> Death has left us without a leader,
> Grandsire Gyamfi Amoyaw of Wonoo.
> He has died and left us without a leader.
> Alas, mother! Alas, father!
> Alas, mother! Alas, father!
> Grandsire Gyamfi Amoyaw, he hails from Wonoo,
> Grandsire Gyamfi Amoyaw,
> He has died and left us without a leader.
> We are being carried away.

1. Idowu 1962, p.191.
2. Nketia 1955, p.122.

Death is carrying us all away.

Grandsire Gyamfi Amoyaw of Wonoo,

He hails from Wonoo, Grandsire Gyamfi Amoyaw.

Death is carrying us all away.

Alas mother! Alas, father!

Grandsire Gyamfi Amoyaw of Wonoo,

He hails from Wonoo, Grandsire Gyamfi Amoyaw,

Death is carrying us all away.

150 | Wait Awhile in Life[1]

This prayer accompanies the rite called Omakola among the Ambo of South West Africa. The rite is for a sick person. The diviner beats calabashes while the people dance. 'Bubble bubbling' refers to a raindrop falling into a puddle, an omen of the day of death. God is referred to as Pamba and Kalunga.

Bubble bubbling from the sky,

We are going to meet with Pamba;

We are going to encounter Kalunga.

I ask the day I am going to die.

I said, 'It will be tomorrow'.

But he said, 'Wait a bit,

So that you may have a big grave made;

Wait awhile in life,

So that you may have a hole scraped out well,

And a grave with a poisonous mushroom growing out of it,

And a tomb with fungus growing out of it.'

151 | God, You Have Called Too Soon[2]

The first part of this Ambo prayer from South West Africa is addressed

---

1. Dymond 1950, p.147.
2. Dymond 1950, p.148.

to God, the master of death, but the people lament his taking their friend too soon. The second part of the prayer is addressed to the departed, asking him to prepare a place for them.

> Would it were not today!
> God, you have called too soon!
> Give him water, he has left without food;
> Light a fire, he must not perish of cold.
>
> Prepare a place for us.
> In a little while we shall reach you.
> Let us reach each other.

152 | Give Me Another Year, Lord[1]

These short, religious choruses were recorded from the Aladura Church in West Africa. They occur during a service. The first chorus is a petition for life, while the second stresses the need for continual preparedness.

> Jesus, you know, you know my name,
> Give me another year, O Lord.
> Do Lord, remember me.
> You pray for me and I'll pray for you.

> ———

> Are you ready when the Lord shall come?
> Are you ready when the Lord shall come?
> In the morning, five o'clock,
> In the morning, six o'clock.
> Are you ready when the Lord shall come?

1. Turner 1967, p.113.

BIBLIOGRAPHY

AAFJES, B. *De Blinde Harpenaar,* Amsterdam, 1955.

ABIMBOLA, P. 'Yoruba Oral Literature', *African Notes,* II, 1965, pp.2–3.

ABRAHAM, W. E. *The Mind of Africa,* London, 1962.

ACHEBE, C. *No Longer At Ease,* London, 1960.

————. *The Arrow of God,* London, 1964.

AGUNWA, C. *More Than Once,* London, 1967.

ANONYMOUS. 'Structures fondamentales de a prière Négro-Africaine', *Personnalité Africaine et Catholicisme, (Présence Africaine),* Paris, 1962, pp.91–137.

BALTHASAR, U.VON. *Prayer,* London, 1961.

BASTIDE, R. 'L'expression de la prière chez les peuples sans écriture', *La Maison Dieu,* no.109 1972, pp.98–112.

BEATTIE, J. and MIDDLETON, J.(eds.). *Spirit Mediumship and Society in Africa,* London, 1969.

BEIER, U. (ed.). *African Poetry,* Cambridge, 1966.

————. *Yoruba Poetry,* Cambridge, 1970.

BERGOUNIOUX, F. M. and GOETZ, J. *Prehistoric and Primitive Religions,* London, 1966.

BERNARDI, B. *The Mugwe, A Failing Prophet,* Oxford, 1959.

BLEEK, D. F. 'Bushman Folklore' *Africa,* II, 1929, p.306

BLEEK, W. H. I. and LLOYD, L. C. *Specimens of Bushman Folklore,* London, 1911.

BRAIN, J. L. 'Ancestors as Elders in Africa—Further Thoughts', *Africa,* XLIII, 2, 1973, pp.108–133.

BUSIA, K. A. 'The Ashanti', in *Forde 1954,* Oxford, pp.190–209.

CLARKE J. D. 'Ifa Divination', *Journal of the Royal Anthropological Institute,* LXIX, 1939, p.248.

COOK, D. *Origin East Africa,* London, 1965.

DAMMAN, E. *Die Religionen Afrikas,* Stuttgart, 1962.

DICKSON, K. A. and ELLINGWORTH, P. (eds.). *Biblical Revelation and African Beliefs,* London, 1969.

DIETERLEN G. *Les Ames des Dogon* Paris, 1941.

DOUGLAS, M. *Natural Symbols,* London, 1970.

DUNDAS, C. *Kilimanjaro and Its Peoples,* London, 1968 (new impression, original edition 1924.)

DYMOND, G. W. 'The Idea of God in Ovamboland, South West Africa', in *Smith 1950,* pp.135–161.

DYSON-HUDSON, N. *Karimojong Politics,* Oxford, 1966.

EDWARDS, P. *West African Narrative,* London, 1963.

ELIADE, M. *From Primitives to Zen,* London, 1967.

EVANS-PRITCHARD, E. E. Y. *Nuer Religion,* Oxford, 1956.

————. *The Comparative Method in Social Anthropology,* (Hobhouse Memorial Trust Lecture no.33) London, 1963.

EZEANYA, S. N. 'God, Spirits and the Spirit World', in *Dickson and Ellingworth 1969* pp.30–191.

FIELD, M. J. *Religion and Medicine of the Ga People,* Oxford, 1937.

FINNEGAN, R. *Oral Literature in Africa*, Oxford, 1970.

FORDE, D. (ed.). *African Worlds*, Oxford, 1954.

FORTES, M. and DIETERLEN, G. (eds.). *African Systems of Thought*, London, 1965.

GUILLEBAUD, R. 'The Idea of God in Ruanda-Urundi', in *Smith 1950*, pp.180–200.

HARRIS, W. T. The Idea of God Among the Mende', in *Smith 1950*, pp.283 ff.

HARWOOD, A. *Witchcraft, Sorcery and Social Categories*, Oxford, 1970.

HEILER, F. *Prayer: A Study in the History and Psychology of Religion*, (tr. McComb, S. and Park J. E.) London, 1932.

HOLLINGS, M. and GULLICK, E. (eds.). *The One Who Listens*, Southend 1971.

HOLLIS, A. C. *The Nandi-Their Language and Folklore*, Oxford, 1909.

IDOWU, E. B. *Olódùmaré, God in Yoruba Belief*, London, 1962.

————. *African Traditional Religion, A Definition*, London, 1973.

JUNOD, H. A. *The Life of a South African Tribe*, 2 vols. London, 1913.

KACHINGWE, A. *No Easy Task*, London, 1966.

KAYOYA M. *Sur les Traces de Mon Père*, Bujumbura, 1968.

KENYATTA, J. *Facing Mount Kenya*, London, 1938.

————. *My People of Kikuyu*, Nairobi, 1966.

KONADU, A. *A Woman in her Prime*, London, 1967.

LIENHARDT, R. G. *Divinity and Experience*, Oxford, 1961.

LINDBLOM, C. *The Akamba of British East Africa*, Uppsala, 1920.

LITTMANN, E. *Galla Verskunst*, Tübingen, 1925.

MARSHALL, L., 'Kung Bushman Religious Beliefs', *Africa*, XXXII, 1962, p. 247 ff.

MAURIER, H. *The Other Covenant: A Theology of Paganism*, New York, 1968.

MAWINZA, J. 'Reverence for Ancestors in Tanzania, with Reference to the Luguru and Other Bantu Tribes', in *Theory and Practice in Church Life and Growth* (mimeographed) Nairobi, 1968, p.44 ff.

MBITI, J. S. *African Religions and Philosophy*, London, 1969.

————. *Concepts of God in Africa*, London, 1970.

MODUPE, PRINCE. *I Was a Savage*, New York, 1950.

MOREAU, J. 'Les Pygmées'. *Parole et Mission*, XI, 1960, p.548.

NADEL S. F. *A Black Byzantium*, Oxford, 1942.

————. *Nupe Religion*, London, 1954.

NGUGI, J. 'The Fig Tree', in *Cook 1965*, pp.70–76.

NKETIA, J. H. *Funeral Dirges of the Akan People*, Achimota, 1955.

————. *Drumming in the Akan Communities of Ghana*, London, 1963.

NYOM, B. 'Le Sacré et l'Unité de l'Homme chez les Bantou du Sud-Caméroun', (doctoral thesis), Lille, 1964.

OKOT p'BITEK. *The Religion of the Central Luo*, Nairobi, 1971.

PARRINDER, E. G. 'The Theistic Beliefs or the Yoruba and Ewe Peoples of West Africa', in *Smith 1950*, p.233 ff.

————. *African Traditional Religion*, Oxford, 1952.

————. *Religion in Africa*, Harmondsworth, 1969

PARSONS, R. T. *Religion in an African Society*, Leiden, 1964.

PASTORAL INSTITUTE OF EASTERN AFRICA. 'Divinity, Prayer and Oathing', Gaba, 1970 (mimeographed).

PAWELZIK, F. *Afrika Bidt*, s'Gravenhage, 1968.

Personnalité Africaine et Catholicisme, see Anonymous.

POSSELT, F. W. T. *Fact and Fiction*, Bulawayo, 1942.

READ, M. *The Ngoni of Nyasaland*, London, 1956.

ROSCOE, J. *The Bakitara or Banyoro*, Cambridge, 1923.

SANGREE W. H. *Age, Prayer and Politics in Tiriki, Kenya*, Oxford, 1966.

SAWYERR, H. *God Ancestor or Creator ?*, London, 1970.

SCHMIDT, W. *Der Ursprung der Gottesidee*, vol. VI, 1933.

————. *Der Ursprung der Gottesidee*, vol. VIII, 1949.

SELIGMAN, C. G. and B. Z. *The Pagan Tribes of the Nilotic Sudan*, London, 1932.

SHORTER, A. 'The Word That Lives, An Anthology of African Prayers' Gaba, 1970 (mimeographed).

————. 'Prayer in African Tradition', *African Ecclesiastical Review*, no.1, 1972, pp.11–17.

————. *Chiefship in Western Tanzania*, Oxford, 1972.

SMITH, E. W. (ed.) *African Ideas of God*, London, 1950.

————. 'The Idea of God Among South African Tribes' in *Smith 1950*, pp.78–134.

STAPPERS, L. 'Prayer of a Milembwe Woman After a Child's Birth', *Kongo-Overzee*, vol. 18, 1952, pp.6–7.

SUNDKLER, B. G. M. *Bantu Prophets in South Africa*, Oxford, 1948.

TAYLOR, J. V. *The Primal Vision*, London, 1963.

TRILLES, R. P. 'Les Pygmées de la Forêt Equatoriale', *Anthropos. Coll.* vol. III, no.4, 1932.

TURNER, H. W. *African Independent Church*, Oxford, 1967.

TUTSCHEK, C. *A Grammar of the Galla (Boran) Language*, Munich, 1845.

WAGNER, G. *The Bantu of North Kavirondo*, Oxford, 1949.

————. 'The Abaluyia of Kavirondo', in *Forde 1954*, p.44.

WESTERMANN, D. *The Shilluk People*, Berlin, 1912.

WILLIAMSON, S. G. 'The Lyric in the Fante Methodist Church', *Africa*, XXVIII, 1958, p.129.

WILSON, M. *Rituals of Kinship Among the Nyakyusa*, Oxford, 1957.

————. *Communal Rituals of the Nyakyusa*, Oxford, 1959.

WING, J.VAN. 'Bakongo Incantations and Prayers', *Journal of the Royal Anthropological Institute*, LX, 1930, pp.418–19.

YOKOO, S. 'Death Among the Abaluyia'. (diploma dissertation), Kampala, 1966.

YOUNG, T. C. *Contemporary Ancestors*, London, 1940.

————. 'The Idea of God in Northern Nyasaland', in *Smith 1950*, p.44 ff.

Prepared for press, designed and published by Oxford University Press, Electricity House, Harambee Avenue, P.O. Box 72532, Nairobi, Kenya, and Printed by Kenya Litho Ltd., Changamwe Road, P.O. Box 40775, Nairobi.